Exodus from Scratch

Available in the Bible from Scratch Series

The Bible from Scratch: The Old Testament for Beginners
Genesis from Scratch: The Old Testament for Beginners
Exodus from Scratch: The Old Testament for Beginners
The Bible from Scratch: The New Testament for Beginners
Matthew's Gospel from Scratch: The New Testament for Beginners
Mark's Gospel from Scratch: The New Testament for Beginners
Luke's Gospel from Scratch: The New Testament for Beginners

Exodus from Scratch

The Old Testament for Beginners

Donald L. Griggs
W. Eugene March

WESTMINSTER JOHN KNOX PRESS
LOUISVILLE • KENTUCKY

First edition
Published by Westminster John Knox Press
Louisville, Kentucky

13 14 15 16 17 18 19 20 21 22—10 9 8 7 6 5 4 3 2

Book design by Teri Kays Vinson
Cover design by Dilu Nicholas

Library of Congress Cataloging-in-Publication Data

Griggs, Donald L.
    Exodus from scratch : the Old Testament for beginners / Donald L. Griggs, W. Eugene March.
       p. cm.
    Includes bibliographical references.
    ISBN 978-0-664-23675-5 (alk. paper)
    1. Bible. O.T. Exodus—Commentaries. I. March, W. Eugene (Wallace Eugene), 1935– II. Title.
    BS1245.53.G75 2013
    222'.1207—dc23

                         2012032922

Most Westminster John Knox Press books are available at special quantity discounts when purchased in bulk by corporations, organizations, and special-interest groups. For more information, please e-mail SpecialSales@wjkbooks.com.

Contents

Contents

Part One

PARTICIPANT'S GUIDE

W. EUGENE MARCH

Preface to Part One

A story of liberation from harsh slavery, a drama of moral power against immoral power, an account of human weakness and strength, and much more—that is what the book of Exodus offers the attentive reader.

The book of Exodus was constructed from a vast collection of available traditions to present the story of a people who began as an unknown clan and became the nucleus of a nation that would have a history in the Middle East lasting for over a millennium. The process of developing the story itself covered a period of some four hundred years. Several different collectors and editors worked to shape the final account, and there are a number of places where their work is obvious. Nonetheless, the narrative is now a whole and is fascinating to read and to discuss.

In preparing this study, I had to face several facts, each of which required a decision. First, forty chapters is too much to consider in seven lessons. Of course, the study could have been longer, but this is intended as an introduction, a glimpse into material that I hope the reader will engage more deeply in subsequent study. To achieve a reasonable length for consideration, I had to be selective about what to present. There are whole chapters that I have omitted altogether. There are others where I more or less summarized parts so as to concentrate on smaller sections.

Second, this study is intended to acquaint the reader with the literary character of the book of Exodus. The story line is exciting. The imagery is at times startling and even offensive, but I have tried to preserve it as best I could. That means there are places where the original language of the text, Hebrew, has to be considered. There is no substitute for reading the text of Exodus itself and becoming thoroughly acquainted with its literary character. Themes reoccur, terminology is used repeatedly, and characters develop. While the text has been stylized in places, Exodus preserves stories about human struggles and achievements that can still stir imagination and hope. To notice these things is to be enriched.

Finally, this is an ancient text from a distant time and place. The authors made no attempt to write an "objective" history (even if that were possible), but it has been necessary at times for me to present some archaeological, historical, sociological, and literary background to enable the reader to better understand the material at hand. There is always the danger of getting too technical and too pedantic. There is so much critical background that I wanted to share, but I have tried to avoid getting bogged down. Balance is what I sought and, I hope, maintained.

I must confess up front that I do not read the Bible as I read most other literature. I read the Bible with the conviction that there is a God who cares for humankind and with the expectation that through the words of the Bible, God can still communicate with us. Thus, as I read I am asking not only the literary and historical questions that I bring to other things I read. I am also reflecting on how this story challenges my understanding of life and how I am to act. I certainly do not accept uncritically everything I read in the Bible, but I do assume that what is there has a purpose that may well help me grow and mature as I "write" my own personal story. I read the Bible fully aware of its human character—as a book written by real people for real people—but I also listen for another voice, a divine voice. My presentations will no doubt reflect this bias on occasion.

I hope three things for the reader of this study. First, I hope you will find the book of Exodus as intriguing as I do. The worldview of the narrative is so different that it will take imagination and patience to enter it fully, but I hope you take the time to do so. Second, I hope that you gain a greater appreciation for and interest in a more careful study of the Bible as a whole. The more one delves into this literature, the richer the material and the greater the reward. Third, the best study of the Bible is done in community with others. There is a wide fellowship of biblical readers (Christian, Jewish, Muslim) who continue to invite others to join with them. I hope you will find a company of folk who will help you in your study even as you enrich theirs.

Study Exodus carefully and with openness. There is much here that can challenge and transform the attentive student. Enjoy!

Chapter One

In Pharaoh's Egypt

A Study of Exodus 1:1–2:25

The book of Exodus begins with a people oppressed by slavery and concludes with a people delivered into freedom. In it, the two most defining events in Israel's history are recounted: Israel's escape from Egypt and Israel's covenant with God. The major human "hero" of the book, Moses, moves from near death as an infant, to flight as a murderer, to life as an undocumented resident among people not his own, to God's designated leader and interpreter—all in forty chapters. The book of Exodus is central to the faith of Israel and to Judaism, and it is held in high esteem by Christians as well. This one book provides a prism through which the biblical story is to be interpreted.

A Word about the Sources of the Story

The name "Exodus" comes from the earliest Greek translation of the Old Testament (called the Septuagint and widely used by the early Christians, who were mostly Greek speakers), which called the book *Exodos Aigyptou*, or "Exodus from Egypt." In the Hebrew original (and in contemporary Jewish

Bibles), however, the title of the book, in the custom of antiquity, is derived from the opening words of the book, "These are the names" (Hebrew: *ve'eleh shemoth*) and is shortened simply to *Shemoth*, or "Names."

Along with Genesis, the first book of the Bible, Exodus brings together a variety of traditions. During the twentieth century, biblical scholars wrote of four sources—J, E, P, and D—each of which had a distinct character. This was called the documentary hypothesis, and it has been greatly modified since it was proposed. It is enough now to know that there were two basic phases in the development of Exodus. The first came around the time of King David and King Solomon or shortly thereafter, roughly between 950 and 850 BCE. The second came sometime in the sixth century after the destruction of Jerusalem by the Babylonians in 587 BCE.

The narrative of Exodus is part of a longer story that includes Leviticus and Numbers. Sometime after the basic narrative of Exodus was completed, the books of Genesis, Exodus, Numbers, and Leviticus were brought together with the book of Deuteronomy to form what Jews call the Torah and Christians call the Pentateuch. This was the first part of the Bible to be recognized as an authoritative canon. The final edition of the Torah was completed sometime between 525 and 450 BCE.

Egypt the Superpower

Egypt is known by most people today as the land of the pyramids. These remarkable architectural and engineering monuments stand as a reminder of a period long gone when there was a different set of rich and dominant nations. The Egyptians excelled in mathematics and astronomy. The "pyramid age" lasted for some five hundred years (roughly 2600 to 2100 BCE) during the Old Kingdom. It was a time of political stability accompanied by increasing wealth. Eventually, though, the fortunes of Egypt declined. For the five hundred years following the end of the Old Kingdom, Egypt was only moderately powerful in the region.

The New Kingdom, which lasted from around 1550 to 1069 BCE, carried out the next major expansion of Egyptian rule. The events recounted in the book of Exodus most likely occurred in this period. Egypt was the superpower that dominated the area from Nubia in the south (not quite to modern Ethiopia) to the River Euphrates in the north. The area we know as Turkey was also under Egyptian hegemony. A number of city-states loyal to Egypt, such as Ugarit, Tyre, and Megiddo, dotted the landscape. Egypt's dominance as an empire was unchallenged until the end of the twelfth century.

We cannot date the events of Exodus precisely, however, because the Bible does not name any specific Egyptian king by name. The general title "Pharaoh" (which literally meant "big house," somewhat like our use of the term "White House" to refer to the presidential administration) designated the ruler with whom Moses and Israel had to deal. Like our term "president," "Pharaoh" was used of a number of different people. Further, Egyptian records make no mention of Moses and the escape of Israel.

Despite the lack of concrete evidence to prove the case conclusively, Ramses II seems the most likely candidate for the Pharaoh mentioned in Exodus. He had a very long reign (1290 to 1224 BCE). His capital was located in the Delta, where the Israelites seem to have lived. What's more, he carried out an ambitious public building program that may well have involved the Israelites as laborers. After the reign of Ramses II, Egypt slowly but steadily declined in influence, eventually giving way to Assyria and then Babylonia as the dominant power in the Middle East.

Life in Pharaoh's Egypt

Israel's life in Egypt began on a positive note. At the end of Genesis we learned that Jacob (whose other name was Israel: Gen. 32:28) had brought his family to Egypt during a severe famine in Canaan. Things had gone well, and the family had grown significantly (Exod. 1:7). This was in keeping with the promise that God had made to Jacob (Gen. 35:11). But then, records Exodus, a "new king arose over Egypt, who did not know Joseph" (1:8). Joseph was one of Jacob's sons, and he had reached a position of prominence and power in the royal court (Gen. 41:37–57). With Joseph's death and the change in the Egyptian court, life for the people Israel took a negative turn (Exod. 1:6, 8).

Because the Israelites had grown great in number, the new king considered them a threat. He worried that they might participate in a revolt or join with enemies of the court in a time of war. Even more, they might escape and thereby deprive Egypt of the cheap labor on which it depended (1:9–10). Thus, he ordered that the Hebrews be forced into laboring on the construction of Pithom and Ramses, two large supply centers (1:11). Before this, the Israelites had lived as shepherds caring for their flocks and herds and offering assistance in caring for Pharaoh's livestock (Gen. 47:1–12). Out of fear, however, the new Pharaoh changed all that, and the Egyptians "became ruthless in imposing tasks on the Israelites, and made their lives bitter with hard service in mortar and brick and in every kind of field labor" (Exod. 1:13–14).

Nonetheless, even though life became difficult for the Israelites, they continued to thrive. Their numbers increased, causing all the more dread among the Egyptian authorities (1:12). The size of the group was probably not great by modern standards because two midwives, Shiphrah and Puah, seem to have been sufficient to serve the needs of the community (1:15). The Hebrew text does not make clear whether the two midwives were themselves Hebrews, or whether they were Egyptians who worked with the Hebrews. Whatever the case, these two women were in charge of the delivery of newborns, and the Israelite population was steadily increasing.

The fact that the Israelites were numerous made them a threat to Pharaoh. They were a potential enemy from his point of view, so he set out to relieve his anxiety by instituting a draconian plan: Every male infant born to a Hebrew woman was to be killed at delivery (1:16). Infanticide was imposed as the means for population control. The community was to be weakened by hard labor and sapped of new energy and hope with the massacre of all the newborn sons.

In the midst of this dismal scene, however, emerged a silent but effective protest. The two midwives, Shiphrah and Puah, were on the spot. They were the ones immediately involved in the birthing of the Israelite children. They could be held accountable to the king and were persons of little power within their society. The Israelites might not have liked it had Shiphrah and Puah complied with the royal orders, but they would have understood. What can one do when the most powerful authority of the most powerful nation issues a direct command?

Shiphrah and Puah, however, feared God and decided to disregard Pharaoh's order (1:17). When it became evident that there were a number of Hebrew boys being born into the community, the authorities called the midwives in for questioning. The midwives explained coolly that the Hebrew women were stronger than Egyptian women and were able to complete the birthing before the midwives could arrive (1:19). Thus, they could not execute Pharaoh's command to put the newborn males to death. As an outcome of their regard for God and refusal to bow before the misuse of royal power, the midwives flourished, as did the people (1:20–21). It is interesting to note that their names have been preserved by the tradition while that of the mighty Pharaoh has been lost.

An Ironic Twist and the Rescue of Moses

When Pharaoh's order to the midwives to kill the Hebrews' infant males clearly was not producing the desired results, he issued an all-embracing edict to his people: "Every boy that is born to the Hebrews you shall throw into the Nile, but you shall let every girl live" (1:22). Thereby the scene is set for the dramatic rescue of a Hebrew boy who will become, by God's power, the rescuer of his people from Egypt.

With great sparseness of detail, the birth of one of the most significant biblical figures of Israel's history is announced. For all Pharaoh's oppression, the ordinary acts of life continued. In the midst of the ongoing turmoil that had become their lot, two unnamed Levites married (2:1). In due time, a boy was born. His mother hid him for three months (2:2). Then, under the royal threat of harboring a Hebrew baby boy, she put the baby into a basket made watertight in the same way that Noah's ark had been prepared (2:3; Gen. 6:14). She then placed it among the reeds (Hebrew: *suph*) of the Nile (2:3). Later in the book of Exodus, Israel will escape through the Sea of Reeds (Hebrew: *suph*), erroneously interpreted as the "Red" Sea (15:4).

Of course, the mother of this infant boy did not know what would happen, but she did what she could to give the child a chance of survival. In fact, she may have been shrewder than the story at first glance indicates. Had the Hebrew mother strategically set the basket afloat in the hope that an Egyptian woman would discover the baby and have pity? We do not know what the mother's plan included, but the rescue of the baby did in fact occur, and that is where the great irony begins.

Of the possible people who could have been walking by the river, it happened that the daughter of Pharaoh came to bathe at the very place where the basket had been placed (2:5). Was this just an accident, or was it part of the mother's plan? Whichever it was, when the royal princess saw the baby and had the child brought to her, the great ironic twist began (2:5). She recognized the child to be one of the Hebrew babies that her father had designated for death, but she took pity on him (2:6). The baby's older sister, whom the mother had stationed by the river to watch her brother, asked whether the princess would like her to get one of the Hebrew women to nurse the baby. The princess said yes, and the girl called her mother. Thus, the Hebrew woman not only nursed the child, her baby, and cared for him, but she also was paid to do so from the royal treasury (2:7–9)! Not only did Pharaoh fail to kill this Hebrew boy; through the intervention of his own daughter, the child, who would grow up to be his nemesis, was saved.

Pharaoh probably had quite a number of daughters, which meant that the activities of one of them could go unnoticed. She took the Hebrew infant as her son, making him a royal prince. She gave him an Egyptian name, Moses, which was commonly used in royal names, such as Thutmose. According to the tradition, she named him Mosheh/Moses because she "drew" (Hebrew: *mashah*) him out of the water (2:10). Though the Hebrew term *mashah* is not etymologically related to the term *Mosheh*, by supplying this Semitic explanation of Moses' name, the story emphatically links him with the people who are his true family and those whom he will rescue from the oppression of Egypt.

A Further Twist in the Story

Moses grew up in Pharaoh's court as an Egyptian. He played with Egyptians. He looked like an Egyptian. Only a few may have known that he was actually a Hebrew who had been adopted into the family when he was an infant. At what point Moses learned of his Hebrew parents and his connection with this people who had been pressed by Pharaoh into forced labor, we are not told, but at some point he did (2:11). To Egyptians and other Hebrews, he appeared to be an Egyptian. But he knew himself to be a Hebrew. "Hebrew" is a term that the Israelites never applied to themselves. It may be related to the term *'Apiru*, which was used in reference to certain landless, stateless aliens who show up in the records of a number of people in the second millennium. These people served as mercenaries, managers, laborers, and in other service positions. Whether the terms are related or not has not been settled among scholars. However that may be, in our text it is the Egyptians who refer to the Israelites, a group of outsiders who certainly shared some of the characteristics of the *'Apiru*, as the Hebrews.

Knowing that he was a Hebrew put Moses in a difficult position. As an adult, he became increasingly aware of the difficulties facing the Hebrew community. How was he supposed to react? As an Egyptian prince, he might have had some influence in the court. Should he have approached those in authority— or at least his adoptive mother—and pleaded for an adjustment in the treatment of the Hebrews? As a Hebrew, should he have renounced his position of privilege and security and taken up residence among his people? What was he to do?

As is often the case, circumstances forced the issue. One day while he was among the Hebrew workers, perhaps exercising some degree of oversight, he saw an Egyptian taskmaster beating a Hebrew. He killed the Egyptian and hid his body in the sand. This was not an act of bravery so much as an act of passion. Moses thought he had gotten away with murder—after all, he had looked around to see if anyone else was present (2:11–12).

The next day, Moses was again among the Hebrew laborers and saw two of them fighting. He intervened, chastising the one who was in the wrong for striking a fellow Hebrew. At that point, the wrongdoer turned on Moses and said, "Who made you a ruler and judge over us? Do you mean to kill me as you killed the Egyptian?" (2:14). Whether the worker understood that Moses was a fellow Hebrew or not is unclear. However that might be, he had witnessed or had heard about Moses' murderous act. If one Hebrew worker knew of the event, Moses surmised, then surely others knew of it as well. It was only a matter of time before Moses' picture would be on a "Wanted" sign and he would be sought by Pharaoh. And so it was (2:15).

An Undocumented Fugitive

Moses did not wait around to see if he could talk his way out of the predicament. He left Egypt, his adoptive mother, his Hebrew parents and the Hebrew community and headed east to the land of Midian (2:15). Midian was a loosely defined territory. It seems basically to have been in the desert regions of the Transjordan, east of the Jordan River and south of the Dead Sea (today the western Arabian Peninsula). The Midianites are variously described as traders (Gen. 37:25–36) and as shepherds (Exod. 2:17). They were probably like some of the Bedouin people still to be found in that region.

Moses decided to settle down in Midian. One day he was at a community well when the seven daughters of the local priest, Reuel (known as Jethro in 3:1 and 18:1 and as Hobab in Num. 10:29, where he is identified as Reuel's son), came to water the family flock. After they had filled the troughs with water, some other shepherds tried to drive the women away so that their own flocks could drink the water. Moses rose to the defense of Reuel's daughters and then helped them by watering their flock (2:16–17). The women returned to their father and reported what had happened. Reuel immediately had Moses brought to eat with the family (2:19–20).

Hospitality among seminomadic peoples is well documented. The peoples of the desert regularly provide lodging and protection to strangers who come their way. As the story goes, Reuel did not ask Moses why, as an Egyptian (2:19), he was wandering about the wilderness frequented by the Midianites. He simply welcomed Moses, at least initially. After some unspecified time, Reuel extended his hospitality by giving his daughter Zipporah to Moses in marriage (2:21).

Moses and Zipporah lived in Midian near or with Reuel for several years. They had a son that Moses named Gershom, a name built on a Hebrew word that was used to identify an alien living in a foreign land (2:22). (Whether or not Gershom is the same son mentioned in 4:25 is debated; see also 4:20 and 18:3–4.) Moses spent some years in Midian tending his father-in-law's flocks (3:1), and perhaps refashioning his self-understanding.

A Cry for Help

Though Moses may have been living a happy life as a resident alien in Midian, most of the Hebrews were still in Egypt, groaning in their slavery. In the midst of great difficulty, the people cried out to God. Their cries were heard by God, says the text, and "God remembered his covenant with Abraham, Isaac, and Jacob" (2:24; see Gen. 17:7–8, 19, 21; 35:11–12; 46:3–4). God had made a commitment to be with this people. Now God "took notice of them" (2:25).

This point in the story signals the content of the remainder of the book: God has heard and God will deliver. The agent of rescue will be Moses, though he does not yet know it. The people will be transformed from a loose collection of Hebrew slaves into a people named Israel. That will be the rest of the story.

Conclusion

In the two opening chapters of Exodus, we have been invited to follow the unfolding of a dramatic story of human liberation. The scene is deftly laid out. There is real human suffering and oppression. There is no "make-believe" here. A cruel national leader has determined, out of fear, to destroy a significant group of people. No pity is to be shown. Then the story takes an unexpected turn when the daughter of the ruler does indeed show pity by rescuing a small Hebrew child from almost certain death. That child grows into manhood, identifies with his people, and then flees as a murderer to find life in a foreign land among a people he had not previously known. All of this is succinctly told with a captivating simplicity. It is recounted to prepare us for the story of what God was about to do in response to the cry of the oppressed for help.

Chapter Two

Who Did You Say You Were?

A Study of Exodus 3:1–6:30

Names are important. In business it is important to remember the names of clients in order to greet them correctly. When musical groups are formed, special care is taken in choosing a memorable name. When a child comes into a family, there is often great deliberation about the name to be given to the child. In social settings, an important skill in making friends and developing relationships is learning and remembering the names of those one meets. The point is clear: names are important.

In ancient Semitic cultures, the importance of names was even greater. In addition to the reasons already suggested, names in Semitic cultures conveyed hopes, convictions, fears, and beliefs. In the Old Testament, for instance, many of the Hebrew names are statements of some sort or another. "Daniel" means "God judges." "Elijah" means "My God is the Lord." "Immanuel" means "God is with us." How a person was named could become a statement about what the parents expected of their child.

The names of people and of places were important. So was the name of God. In today's English-speaking world, most people use the word "God" as if it were a name, but it is a generic term referring to the divine. In ancient Israel,

God had a personal name, just like each of us has a name. To know that name was important. This part of the book of Exodus presents an account of Moses' learning God's name. It is engaging, insightful, and somewhat enigmatic. The issue is simple and yet profound. How should one expect God to answer when asked the question "Who are you?"

Moses Is Encountered by God

The day began in an ordinary manner. Moses took his father-in-law's flock to graze on the slopes of Horeb, the mountain of God, as he had probably done many times before (3:1). In the preceding chapter we were introduced to Moses' father-in-law as Reuel ("friend of God"), father of Zipporah ("little bird"), a priest of the Midianites. He is now identified with the name Jethro ("excellence"). The difference in names may reflect the existence of two different traditions about this man so important in Moses' story.

In this account, "the mountain of God" is called Horeb. It is more widely known in the Bible as Sinai. (This also probably reflects the existence of at least two different traditions.) Its location is never precisely defined. A number of mountains have been suggested as *the* mountain, but the evidence is mixed. Of the two most widely held candidates for the location, one is somewhere in northwest Arabia (where Midian is thought to have been located), and the other is in the southern end of the Sinai Peninsula (where Christian interpreters as early as the fourth century identified Jebel Musa as the site). Biblical evidence can be cited in support of each.

Wherever Horeb was, Moses was there tending Jethro's flock. Suddenly, the normalcy of the day ended. Moses saw a bush of the kind that flourishes in the semiarid region. It was aflame, but the fire was not devouring it. That would have been strange enough, but the narrator adds that "the angel of the Lord appeared to him in the flame" (3:2). Even more disconcerting, we are told nothing more concerning this divine intermediary. The angel said nothing and made no gesture; it just appeared. Two verses later, however, it is God, not an "angel of the Lord," who spoke from the bush to a puzzled and awed Moses (3:4).

When Moses turned aside to take a closer look at the strange sight, God intercepted him with the command to approach no closer and to remove his sandals from his feet, telling him that "the place on which you are standing is holy ground" (3:5). God then announced, "I am the God of your father, the God of Abraham, the God of Isaac, and the God of Jacob" (3:6). This self-identification by God makes clear that the God whom the forebears encountered in the book of Genesis is the God who addressed Moses. That is important for two reasons. First, in terms of the Moses story, there is no reason to assume that he knew much about the traditions of his Hebrew family. He had been raised as an Egyptian. He knew he had an ethnic connection to the Hebrews, but he may well have been ignorant of the traditions of his forebears.

The second reason that the self-identification of God is important becomes immediately clear. Moses' people in Egypt were no strangers to God. God called them "my people." God had "observed the misery of my people who are in Egypt" (3:7). They had not been abandoned. God intended to lead them out of Egypt and into the "land flowing with milk and honey" as promised to the forebears (3:8–9; see Gen. 15:19–21; 17:8; 35:11–12). And how was this to take place? Moses was to be God's agent of deliverance. God had chosen Moses to return to Egypt, to confront Pharaoh, and to lead the Hebrews out of their suffering and into the land promised to the ancestors so many generations earlier (3:10).

God's Name Revealed

One might think that Moses would be completely overwhelmed by this experience. Challenged by God himself, Moses stood on a deserted mountainside with nothing more concrete before him than a flaming bush that was not consumed. What would you do in such a circumstance? If he had fainted or just turned away or simply said, "Yes, Lord," that would be understandable. But that is not what happened.

No, Moses dared to ask God a question: "Who am I that I should go to Pharaoh, and bring the Israelites out of Egypt?" (3:11). After all, Moses was a wanted man in Egypt. He had been in Midian for some time. He had a wife and several sons (4:20), and a place in the Midianite community. He had little direct connection with the Israelites. Why should he go back to Egypt? Then the clincher: "If I come to the Israelites and say to them, 'The God of your ancestors has sent me to you,' and they ask me, "What is his name?' what shall I say to them?" (3:13). Moses did not think he had a chance at all against Pharaoh. Further, he did not even know for sure who it was—this one speaking from the burning bush—that wanted him to return to Egypt. Moses wanted answers.

God responded by assuring Moses that the divine presence would accompany him. The sign that all events to take place would be God's doing would occur when Moses had brought the Israelites out of Egypt to worship on the very mountain where he stood (3:12). But God went further. God revealed to Moses the divine name. Remember how important names were in antiquity. God said to Moses, "I AM WHO I AM" (3:14). Moses was to tell the Israelites that "I AM has sent me to you" (3:14). The narrator continues: "Thus you shall say to the Israelites, 'The LORD, the God of your ancestors, the God of Abraham, the God of Isaac, the God of Jacob has sent me to you': This is my name forever, and this my title for all generations" (3:15).

The traditional English rendering of the text as "I AM" is based on the Greek translation, the Septuagint. The Hebrew phrase involved, however, can better be translated, "I will be what I will be" or "I will bring to pass what I will bring to pass." The Hebrew verb in question is *'ehyeh*, the first-person singular imperfect form of the root *hayah,* which usually is translated as "he became" or "he caused to happen." The explanation of the personal name of God centers on this first-person verbal form in this passage ("I am" in Greek; "I become" or "I cause to happen" in Hebrew), but the form of the personal name of God found most often in the biblical text is YHWH.

We can only make an educated guess about the pronunciation of YHWH because sometime in the early part of the Common Era Jews quit pronouncing the name. This was done as a sign of reverence: one did not call the Sovereign of the universe by a personal name. When the Bible was read or when prayers were said in worship, the readers substituted "Lord" or "the Holy One" or "the Name" for YHWH. The consonants in the Hebrew text were given vowels that represented one of the substitute names that one was to say instead of the now sanctified, unpronounceable YHWH. Today scholars, on the basis of names like Elijah ("My God is Yah") or terms like "hallelujah" ("Praise Yah"), surmise the name might have been pronounced "Yahweh," but we do not know for certain. The King James Version (KJV) used "Jehovah" to represent YHWH in some places and "the LORD" in most places, while the New Revised Standard Version (NRSV) and most other recent English translations insert "the LORD" whenever the text has YHWH (3:15).

When we see that God did have a personal name and that this name was supposedly revealed to Moses at the burning bush, the case for multiple sources of tradition is strengthened. Even before the passage in Exodus that we are considering, there are numerous places in the preceding chapters of the Bible where God is already known as YHWH (e.g., Gen. 2:4–22; 12:1; 18:1; 21:1). Thus, the revelation of a name already known in the tradition seems a little curious. One can always explain the current context as being necessary simply because Moses and his generation didn't know the name YHWH (see 6:3). But the way the narrative is developed, it seems to want us to believe that this was the very first time that anyone learned of God's personal name. This account suggests that the name YHWH was the special knowledge of Moses and thereby a source of power. That might be so at one level, but the storytellers of earlier times certainly knew and used the personal name YHWH in reference to God.

Moses' Problem with the Israelites

There were two targets for the message that Moses was directed to convey: the Israelites and Pharaoh. Each was difficult in its own way. With regard to sharing

God's message with the oppressed Israelites living in Egypt, Moses anticipated two problems. First, the people would not even know who he was. After all, he had been raised as an Egyptian and had been in Midian for a number of years. Second, Moses did not consider himself impressive as an orator (4:10). When he protested to God about this, God responded, "Who gives speech to mortals? Who makes them mute or deaf, seeing or blind? Is it not I the LORD? Now go, and I will be with your mouth and teach you what you are to speak" (4:11–12). When Moses continued his objection, God declared to Moses that his brother Aaron, who could "speak fluently," would "serve as a mouth for you and [that] you [would] serve as God for him" (4:16). God told Moses to hear God's words and then share them with Aaron: "Put the words in his mouth; and I will be with your mouth and with his mouth, and will teach you what you shall do" (4:15).

Perhaps even more problematic, however, was the basic attitude of the people. It is always difficult to move from what is known, even if it is unpleasant, to what is unknown. The Israelites had been in Egypt for over four hundred years (12:40). Their current situation was not good, but there had been other Pharaohs under whom life had been reasonable. They were not at all sure about this man who had emerged from the wilderness. In somewhat the same way that the Hebrew workman fighting with one of his fellows had earlier questioned Moses' authority (2:13–14), the question for the Israelites was, "Who made you our leader?"

God instructed Moses to tell the people of his experience on Horeb, about the encounter he had had with God. Moses was to declare the divine name, YHWH, and assure the elders and the people that God had sent Moses to them (3:14). God had heard the cry of the people and had remembered the covenant made with their forebears (3:7–10). The generation of Israelites to whom Moses was sent may not have remembered or even known that God had a long-standing relationship with their ancestors. The news that God intended to "deliver them from the Egyptians" (3:8) may well have been heard with a degree of skepticism. How much misery would they have to experience before God would act? If God cared for them, why was such a situation allowed to develop? Moreover, Pharaoh was no pushover. Such questions are still raised in light of the turmoil, injustice, and suffering so obvious around the world.

Moses himself remained just a little skeptical. Why should the leaders of the Israelites accept him as God's envoy? What if they disputed his claim that God had appeared to him (4:1)? The response was immediate and direct: God gave three signs to Moses. First, Moses was instructed to throw his staff to the ground. When he did, the staff became a snake. When he picked it back up, it was a staff again (4:2–5). Next, Moses' hand became "leprous" and then returned to normal (4:6–7). Finally, Moses would be able to take water from the Nile and pour it on dry land, where it would become blood (4:8–9). This was apparently enough to convince Moses to return to Egypt. As the story unfolded,

---

however, the people continued to question Moses' leadership for some time to come (6:12). We will return to this theme later.

Moses' Problem with the Pharaoh

The other target for Moses' message was Pharaoh. He was the toughest nut to crack. He was not accustomed to having people order him about. He was particularly unprepared to have this Midianite nut Moses, and his Israelite friends, tell him what he should do. Pharaoh responded skeptically: "Who is the LORD [YHWH], that I should heed him and let Israel go? I do not know the LORD [YHWH], and I will not let Israel go" (5:2). Pharaoh's reaction concerning a supposed message from God was clear: Who did you say you were? Who is YHWH anyway? Convincing Pharaoh was no easy task.

To allow the members of a major labor force to wander off for a "Labor Day" festival in honor of a deity unknown to Pharaoh was out of the question (3:18; 4:22–23; 5:1), so Pharaoh instructed his taskmasters to increase the workload for the Israelites. The quota of brick the Hebrews were expected to produce daily remained the same, but the straw necessary for making the bricks was no longer to be provided (5:6–13). Instead, the workers had to find their own supply of straw. When the task was not completed, the Israelite supervisors appointed by the Egyptians were beaten (5:14). When they sought relief from Pharaoh for the unjust treatment they received, Pharaoh scornfully called them "lazy" and sent them back to their task (5:15–19). More, much more was going to be necessary before Pharaoh would change his position regarding the Hebrews.

God's Assurance to Moses

When the Israelites could get no relief from Pharaoh or his taskmasters, they turned on Moses and Aaron. They blamed the two brothers for bringing them "into a bad odor with Pharaoh" and for bringing them to the edge of the sword (5:20–21). The people still did not really believe that God had sent Moses. They had trusted for a brief time when Aaron, at Moses' direction, performed a series of wondrous signs before them. They had listened in awe to the message that God had seen their misery and was about to act (4:29–31). But that was before they had been confronted with the brutality of Pharaoh, before they were reminded of who seemed to have the real power. "I AM" seemed somewhat distant. YHWH may be the name of God, but where was God's power to protect and preserve?

Moses himself was not sure. He may well have asked God, "Who did you say you were?" He hadn't been looking for God out on Horeb. He was minding his own business when God encountered him and revealed his name to him. Since then, he had had nothing but trouble. Now he was being blamed by the people for what God had done. Moses wanted some answers. "O LORD [YHWH], why have you mistreated this people? Why did you send me?" (5:22). His announcements about God's intentions toward the Israelites had brought them nothing but trouble. If God was so keen on delivering the Israelites, why didn't God do something to help the people out of their dire straights (5:23)?

At this point, God had to start over, giving assurance to Moses by reaffirming his original promise. In a sense, this is what God said: "Look, I meant what I said. You are about to see something extraordinary. I told you at the very beginning that Pharaoh was going to be difficult. Nothing but being hit in the solar plexus by my mighty hand will move that guy. I will have to do some terrible things to Egypt before Pharaoh will let the people go. So get ready, because it is about to happen" [3:19–20; 6:1]. God went on to recall the covenant made with the forebears to give them the land of Canaan (6:4). Now, having heard "the groaning of the Israelites whom the Egyptians are holding as slaves" (6:5), God intended to act.

Moses was once again instructed to tell the Israelites that YHWH was determined to free them from the Egyptians. By the might of God's outstretched arm, God would deliver the Israelites from slavery (6:6). The people would soon be convinced that Moses and Aaron were divinely appointed guides because they would see God's deliverance. They would be claimed by God as God's people, and God would be their God. "You shall know," said God, "that I am the LORD your God, who has freed you from the burdens of the Egyptians. I will bring you into the land that I swore to give to Abraham, Isaac, and Jacob; I will give it to you for a possession. I am the LORD" (6:7–8).

We might think that words such as these would be totally persuasive, but they were not. The Israelites "would not listen to Moses" (6:9). Why not? Because their spirit had been broken. Slavery had reduced them to a people with no hope and no courage and with the inability to trust that things could be better. Convincing the Israelites that it had truly been God who spoke and who was about to act would remain an ongoing task for Moses in the days and years ahead.

God was not going to wait until Pharaoh was willing to cooperate. Moses had a message to deliver to Pharaoh. Understandably, perhaps, Moses remained uncertain. After all, the Israelites had not listened to him; so why should Pharaoh, particularly since Moses considered himself to be such a poor speaker (6:12)? God was growing tired of hearing Moses complain and question his assignment, so God ordered Moses and Aaron to quit delaying their task and go tell Pharaoh to "let the Israelites go out from his land" (6:11). Israel and Pharaoh were yet unconvinced about the God with whom each was dealing. But each was soon to have a definite answer to the question "Who did you say you were?"

Conclusion

Naming was very important in antiquity. The revelation of God's personal name YHWH to Moses was a watershed moment. The stories preserved in the book of Genesis about God's acts of creation and the promises to Abraham, Isaac, and Jacob are irreversibly connected with the deliverance of Israel from Egypt announced by YHWH. Moses was selected and commissioned by God to lead the people out of Egypt. Neither the Israelites nor Pharaoh responded unequivocally in a positive manner. A great struggle pitting Pharaoh against God was about to begin. The outcome would make clear to all that the answer to the question "Who did you say you were?" was YHWH, the promise keeper and deliverer of Israel.

Chapter Three
Let My People Go

A Study of Exodus 7:1–25; 11:1–12:42; 14:1–15:21

The refrain of a well-known African American spiritual states concisely one of the major themes of the book of Exodus:

> Go down Moses, way down in Egypt's land,
> Tell old Pharaoh, Let my people go!

It is a peppy, confident song that one can sing with joy. Liberty, release, deliverance, freedom—that is what was at stake for the Hebrews. Yet today, that hope for the end of injustice continues to motivate oppressed peoples around the globe when they hear the story of Exodus.

There was something else going on in this confrontation with "old Pharaoh," however. In ancient Egypt, Pharaohs were considered by many—particularly by Pharaohs themselves—to be divine. Most of them were men, though there were at least six, and perhaps eight, women who across the centuries were acknowledged as Pharaohs. However much they may have felt divine, they were human beings who ate and slept and did what people do. They exercised sovereignty well sometimes, and not so well at other times. They had numerous people to assist them, but they could and did at times make horrendous errors that usually cost others their lives. Nonetheless, they were considered by some of their subjects to share in the qualities of the divine. They were thus due the lavish lifestyles that most experienced. The pyramids were appropriate locations for these "gods" to be placed as they began their return to their eternal place among the deities who governed the universe.

When YHWH squared off against Pharaoh, then, this was more than just another routine contest. This was not just a game of tag. This was a struggle to determine who actually was God. Pharaoh or YHWH? Who was truly all-powerful and worthy of absolute allegiance? Pharaoh or YHWH? Whom should you worship, and to whom should you entrust your life? Pharaoh or YHWH? The battle was at times brutal and certainly not for the faint of heart. But in the end, the only sovereign ruler of the universe, God Almighty, would prevail.

The Struggle Begins

The message Moses and Aaron had to deliver was quite clear: Pharaoh was to allow the Israelites to leave Egypt. If Pharaoh would not comply, then God intended to force their release by great acts of judgment (7:4). The Egyptians would come to recognize that YHWH was God when the Israelites were brought out of Egypt (7:5). There were to be many "signs and wonders" before the matter would be settled (7:3).

At the outset, however, Pharaoh did not readily yield to Moses. In fact, the text says that God would "harden Pharaoh's heart" so that he would not respond positively to God's instruction (7:3). This is very strange. Why would God purposely render Pharaoh incapable of doing what God wanted him to do? There are two ways of addressing this question. The first has to do with terminology chosen by the translators. In the passage under consideration, three different Hebrew terms are used, all of which are translated in the NRSV with some form of "harden." In 7:3, the Hebrew term connotes a kind of resistance, more on the order of stubbornness than unheeding. "Harden" is a somewhat misleading translation. In 7:13 (as in 4:21; 7:22; 11:10) the Hebrew word literally means "to make strong," which can be understood as "determined" or "certain." It does not mean "harden" and does not necessarily carry a negative connotation of divine disabling. In 7:14, the Hebrew term literally means "heavy." Pharaoh's heart is "heavy" in the sense of being fixed, set, or determined. To choose the one term "harden" as the best translation for these several terms with their varying connotations is problematic.

The Hebrew terminology suggests a picture of Pharaoh as stubborn, fixed in his ideas, unwilling to consider a path different from the one he has chosen. The more resistance Pharaoh received, the more he dug in his heels. The more

Pharaoh refused any relief or any change in his plans, the more resistance he raised. It was a vicious circle that is recounted a number of times in the chapters that follow.

Having considered this, however, the text still leaves the reader with a sense that God somehow knew what Pharaoh would do and, by the very plan chosen, at the very least aggravated the situation. Those who preserved the traditions in the book of Exodus were not overly concerned about the issue of free will that bothers so many contemporary readers. They believed God capable of directing historical events while at the same time allowing for human responsibility. However we resolve this theological enigma, two matters are underscored by the text: first, Pharaoh made his own decisions to challenge God; second, God was recognized from the beginning of the account as the one who would be the ultimate victor in this contest between the "gods."

Signs and Wonders

The contest is described in terms of a series of "signs and wonders" that God directed Moses and Aaron to announce and perform on behalf of God. When Moses and Aaron initially had gone to the Israelites' leaders to make known God's intention to deliver them from their slavery, Moses and Aaron had shown them a number of "signs" to demonstrate God's power (4:3–9, 29–30). In the same way, God was going to multiply God's signs and wonders as the means of convincing Pharaoh to let the Israelites leave Egypt (7:3).

The first phase of the struggle brought Moses and Aaron to the court of Pharaoh to tell him once again to let God's people go. In a remark most likely intended to underscore the seriousness and wisdom of the messengers, we are told that "Moses was eighty years old and Aaron eighty-three when they spoke to Pharaoh" (7:7). In other words, these two were not simply young rabble-rousers out to make a name for themselves. They were mature. They knew the risk they were taking and the possible consequences. Nonetheless, they went before the all-powerful Pharaoh with their message.

In this encounter, at the Lord's instruction, Moses and Aaron were told what to do when Pharaoh ordered them to do a "wonder." Aaron was to throw down Moses' staff before Pharaoh, whereupon it would become a snake. Aaron did as the Lord had instructed, and the rod indeed became a snake (7:9–10). Round 1 goes to God, right? No, because Pharaoh's wise men, sorcerers, and magicians, "by their secret arts," were able to do the same thing (7:11–12). Although Aaron's staff/snake "swallowed up" the others, Pharaoh's mind was already set. Pharaoh "would not listen to them" (7:12–13).

Had Pharaoh not been so obstinate, things might have gone differently. Such was not the case, however. God set out to bring Pharaoh and the Egyptians—and the Israelites for that matter—to the knowledge of who YHWH was. God intended to subdue Pharaoh and put him in his place. Pharaoh, God would demonstrate, was not even close to being divine.

The Struggle Continues

The next episode in this struggle involved a confrontation between Pharaoh and Moses. Moses met Pharaoh, who was taking his morning walk along the bank of the Nile. Moses was to remind Pharaoh that he had been ordered by God to let God's people go, a command Pharaoh had thus far ignored (7:16). Moses was then to strike the water of the Nile with his staff, whereupon the water would turn to blood and all the fish would die (7:17–18). By this sign, God's power was to be displayed.

Moses did as instructed. After delivering his message to Pharaoh, "he lifted up the staff and struck the water in the river, and all the water in the river turned into blood, and all the fish in the river died" (7:20–21). A knockout? No, for once again the Egyptian magicians were able to do the same thing. Thus, Pharaoh remained unconvinced and unimpressed (7:22). The Egyptian populace, however, was beginning to get the message. They had no water to drink and had to deal with the smell of putrefying fish. They could not just walk away as had their Pharaoh (7:21–24).

There were a total of ten such demonstrations before Pharaoh finally gave in. The land was overrun with frogs, then gnats, then flies. The people and their animals were stricken with boils. Next, there was a great hailstorm followed by an infestation of locusts. After all that, a great darkness fell on Egypt, a land where the sun was considered a major deity. The tenth wonder had to do with the death of Egypt's firstborn, a topic to which we will return later. These were terrifying events aimed at bringing Pharaoh to his knees before God, but not until the last did Pharaoh relent and let God's people go.

We must pause here for another word about language. These "signs and wonders" are commonly referred to as "plagues." From our point of view, there was indeed devastation like that experienced by plagues known in modern times. The terrible ravages of the Black Death in the Middle Ages or that of the more recent AIDS virus are what we generally think of when we hear the term "plague." But that word is not actually used in the biblical texts we are considering. There is a term sometimes translated as "plague," but its literal meaning is "to strike." The NRSV correctly translates this term in 7:17 when Moses tells Pharaoh that he is going to "strike" the waters of the Nile. But there is an interpretive jump when in 8:2 the same Hebrew word is rendered as "plague."

The reason for considering this translation issue is that, in our understanding, "plagues" are generally thought to be brought about by natural causes.

Some have interpreted the "signs and wonders" in Exodus along such lines. The Nile is known to sometimes be overtaken with a red algae–like infestation, which in turn might cause the fish to die. Likewise, there are recorded "plagues" of frogs, which in turn might also bring gnats and then flies. And so on. To try to thereby "explain" these "signs and wonders" may make them more believable for modern readers, but such an interpretation completely ignores the repeated insistence in the text that these are God's doings. They are "signs and wonders" by which God intends to convince Pharaoh, the Egyptians, and the Israelites that there is but one sovereign of the universe and that one is YHWH. From the standpoint of the narrators of Exodus, these are miraculous signs performed by Moses and Aaron as enabled by the Lord God, the one who insisted that Pharaoh let God's people go.

The Tenth "Wonder"

The tenth round in the battle of the "gods," Pharaoh against YHWH, was the most terrible of all. At the same time, however, it was the most glorious of all. Let's begin with the tragic side of the story.

In response to Pharaoh's repeated refusal to let God's people go, despite repeated warnings and awesome signs and wonders, the Lord finally announced the final blow ("plague") that Pharaoh and Egypt would receive. Moses warned Pharaoh that God intended to pass through the land of Egypt about midnight and strike down every firstborn in the land: "Every firstborn in the land of Egypt shall die, from the firstborn of Pharaoh who sits on his throne to the firstborn of the female slave who is behind the handmill, and all the firstborn of the livestock" (11:5). The wailing of the bereaved would be great (11:6). But God was going to make certain that the Israelites were left untouched in the midst of all the carnage (11:7). Moses informed Pharaoh that as a result of the disaster, all the king's officials would come and ask Moses and his people to leave Egypt (11:8).

One might think that this would be enough, but God informed Moses, "Pharaoh will not listen to you, in order that my wonders may be multiplied in the land of Egypt" (11:9). Once again we encounter the unsettling and enigmatic comment that the Lord "hardened" Pharaoh's heart so that he would not let the people go (11:10). As noted earlier, the Hebrew term does not literally mean "harden," but what might it mean to say that God "strengthened" Pharaoh's already stubborn resolve? This cannot easily be explained away. There remains a tension between human freedom and responsibility over against the inscrutable plans of God. Both are real; both create the events we call history.

After a break in the narrative about the institution later Judaism has come to know as the Passover, the story continues with the report of the death of all the

Egyptian firstborn, "from the firstborn of Pharaoh who sat on his throne to the firstborn of the prisoner who was in the dungeon" (12:29). Amid the loud cry of lamentation that spread across the land, Pharaoh finally summoned Moses and told him to take the people out of Egypt. God's warning was not enough. The tenth "wonder" had to come about (12:30–31).

The Passover

In the midst of the story of the struggle to free Israel, there is a long pause. Moses and Aaron were given instructions concerning an annual event to be observed by the Israelites. There was to be a sacrifice and a meal, which was to be held on the tenth day of the first month of the year (Hebrew: *Abib* or *Nisan*). In the liturgical calendar, the year began in the spring (12:2–3). This was to be Passover. There was also a civil calendar where the beginning of the year was marked in the fall (Hebrew: *Ethanim* or *Tishri*), the seventh month of the liturgical calendar. Contemporary Jews celebrate the turn of the New Year in the fall and Passover in the spring in accord with the civil calendar.

Explicit instructions were given concerning the ceremony. An unblemished lamb was to be selected on the tenth of the month and then slaughtered at twilight on the fourteenth (12:3–6). A lamb for each family was to be selected, though if a household was small it could join with another in sharing a lamb. The whole lamb was to be roasted over a fire, and all of it was to be eaten or burned up on that night (12:8–10). (Later in the tradition, the feast of Unleavened Bread was connected to the Passover celebration [12:14–20; see also 13:3–10]). The participants were to dress for the meal in preparation for a journey so they could leave hurriedly (12:11). Further, they were to mark each Hebrew home with some of the blood of the sacrificed lamb (12:7). Why? Because when the Lord passed through Egypt to strike down all the firstborn, the inhabitants of the houses marked with blood were to be spared (12:12–13).

The elders of the people did as Moses instructed them. Each house was marked, providing protection for those within (12:21–23). The Israelites were told to "observe this rite as a perpetual ordinance for you and your children" (12:24). When the children in the future asked concerning the rite, the adults were to say, "It is the passover sacrifice to the LORD, for he passed over the houses of the Israelites in Egypt, when he struck down the Egyptians but spared our houses" (12:26–27).

Then the tenth "wonder" occurred. God struck down all the firstborn in Egypt, from the royal house to the prisoners, and from the livestock as well (12:29). There was great distress in the land, and Pharaoh then summoned Moses and Aaron and told them to take their people and leave the land (12:30–31). They did, and they took much wealth with them (12:32-36; see also 3:21–22).

From our vantage point, this divine action may seem too extreme, too harsh, too unfair. It is easy for modern Westerners to feel sympathy for the Egyptians and feel critical of God. But two things must be remembered. First, few North Americans have ever lived under oppressive, cruel taskmasters. Thus, it is difficult for many to hear this text from the standpoint of a victimized, enslaved people. Second, divine judgment in the Bible usually takes the form of God's turning back on a people what they have done to others. Pharaoh tried to wipe the Hebrew community out. The Egyptians were ordered to kill all the firstborn males of the Hebrews (2:18–22). Thus, it is not too harsh for the same penalty to be applied to the Egyptians.

The Exodus

Once Pharaoh capitulated and acknowledged that he was not the supreme deity he once thought he was, the way was clear for Israel to depart from Egypt. There are two accounts of this great event. The older, written in poetry, makes no claim to being "historical" (15:1-18), while the later prose account is written in a style that some have interpreted as literal history (14:1-31). On close scrutiny, however, it seems clear that metaphor and poetic license are used in each account.

In the more ancient of the two celebrations of the departure from Egypt, the Lord is portrayed as a mighty warrior who overthrows the hostile forces (15:2–3). In a brief victory song attributed to Aaron's sister Miriam (which could be the oldest part of the tradition), the theme of the passage is sounded: "Sing to the LORD, for he has triumphed gloriously; horse and rider he has thrown into the sea" (15:20; see 15:1). The "sea" in the Hebrew is the "Sea of Reeds," a marshy area somewhere near where the Suez Canal is now situated. The translators of the Greek Septuagint, many centuries after the Hebrew tradition was first set, interpreted the "sea" as the "Red Sea" (15:4). At any rate, the picture is one of total victory. The "right hand" of the Lord has "shattered the enemy" (15:6). The adversaries are consumed as rubble by fire (15:7). By a "blast" from God's "nostrils" "the floods stood up in a heap; the deeps congealed in the heart of the sea" (15:8). When the enemy sought to pursue the Israelites, God blew the sea back on the Egyptian army: "The sea covered them; they sank like lead in the mighty waters" (15:10). Indeed, "the earth swallowed" the enemy (15:12). This is marvelous, if somewhat contradictory in places, poetic metaphor.

The prose account continues in narrative style to describe the departure of the Israelites. Pharaoh had a change of mind, a renewed "hardening" of his heart, and initiated a pursuit of the people by some part of the Egyptian military (14:5–9). It appeared that the Egyptians had the Israelites trapped between their advancing forces and "the sea," a body of water not at first identified in the Hebrew as the Sea of Reeds (14:2).

The people once again failed in their trust and turned against Moses (14:11–12). Moses said to them, "Do not be afraid, stand firm, and see the deliverance that the LORD will accomplish for you today; for the Egyptians whom you see today you shall never see again. The LORD will fight for you, and you have only to keep still" (14:13–14). The Lord then instructed Moses to stretch out his hand so that the sea would be divided. This is the picture of the Exodus that most people have if they have any at all. The waters formed a wall on either side as the Israelites fled across the dry seabed (14:16, 21–22). When the Egyptian military tried to follow, the waters returned and drowned them all (14:26–28, 30; but see also 25). This is a staggering account that makes a clear point: "The LORD saved Israel that day from the Egyptians" and the "people feared the LORD and believed in the LORD and in his servant Moses" (14:30–31). That was the point of the whole struggle in the first place: to demonstrate who indeed was God. God, YHWH, had prevailed. Pharaoh—no god at all—was vanquished. Deliverance had occurred!

Conclusion

This dramatic story recounts the conflict between the Lord God and Pharaoh. The obstinacy of the Egyptian ruler is matched against the determination of the Lord to set the Israelites free. A number of "signs and wonders" (often called "plagues") are described. Then the climax is reached with the devastation of the Egyptians and the successful escape across the marshy land to Egypt's east. Passover is instituted to serve as a reminder of God's great act of deliverance. What began on a somber note of conflict comes to end with shouts of joy at God's great victory.

Chapter Four

Are We There Yet?

A Study of Exodus 15:22–18:27

After the excitement of the deliverance at the Sea of Reeds, the reality of life on the road set in. The number of people and of their livestock was certainly large, though not the six hundred thousand plus claimed by later tradition (12:37; see also Num. 1:46). They were wandering across a terrain somewhat like that of southern New Mexico and Arizona. They did not know where they were going. They had some food and water when they left Egypt, but it ran out fairly quickly. Providing the bare necessities for life was to be a major challenge. There were no supermarkets in that wilderness, and certainly not the plethora of fast food establishments familiar to modern-day travelers. If you have ever traveled anywhere with children, you can well imagine the nagging that began early on: "Are we there yet? When will we get there? How much longer?" Little did they know at the outset that the trip was going to take some forty years (16:35).

We're Thirsty! Give Us a Drink!

One of the first rules of travel in an arid climate is to stay hydrated by drinking a lot of water. That is possible so long as there is a ready source for that precious

---

liquid. In the desert, though, this can be a real problem. The people had been "on the road" for three days when they reached an oasis named Marah (the exact location of this site is unknown). No doubt they were initially excited at the prospect of having a good, long drink. However, they were quickly disappointed. The place they had reached was named Marah, which means "bitter" in English—and for good reason: the water there was indeed bitter and undrinkable (15:23). We can only imagine how Moses first reacted to this news, but we know very well the reaction of the people: They immediately began to complain against Moses: "What shall we drink?" (15:24). It wasn't as if Moses had purposely arranged this unfortunate circumstance, but he got blamed anyway. Moses in his desperation "cried out to the LORD." What was he to do? God instructed Moses to throw a special kind of "tree" (or bush) into the water. When he did, the water became sweet, refreshing, and life giving (15:25). The people's question was answered. Further, as demonstration of God's care, when the people left Marah, they were guided to Elim, where they found more than enough good water and, as a bonus, plenty of shade (15:27).

While the first crisis was resolved, the need for water continued to be an issue for Moses and the people. At Rephidim, a site as yet unidentified by scholars, the people again quarreled with Moses concerning the lack of water: "Why did you bring us out of Egypt, to kill us and our children and our livestock with thirst?" (17:1–3). Of course, Moses did not intend for the people to be uncomfortable or in distress, but the weary travelers didn't want excuses. They wanted water! Since Moses was in charge, he was, in their minds, responsible for their condition. The people were so worked up about it all that they were almost ready to stone Moses (17:4). The situation was remedied when God instructed Moses to take some of the elders and go on ahead to Horeb. There he was told to strike "the rock at Horeb." When he did, water gushed forth in sufficient quantity "in the sight of the elders of Israel" to relieve the needs of the people (17:5–6).

These two stories describe the hardship of the wilderness wandering, to be sure, but they also draw attention to the lack of confidence that the people had in the whole enterprise. They didn't trust Moses or Aaron to guide them safely through the desert. They were not convinced that the freedom they had been given was worth the difficulties they faced. So they complained and they griped and they stewed about their condition. While they voiced their discontent against Moses, they also expressed doubt about God: "Is the LORD among us or not?" (17:7). The people's lack of trust in God is remembered repeatedly in the stories preserved in Exodus. To a degree, their lack of trust is understandable. They did have some good memories about divine blessings in the past, but that was then. Out in the wilderness, they wanted to ask, "What, God, have you done for us lately?"

God wanted the people to respond by following God's "commandments" and "statutes" (15:26). God wanted them to do what was right in God's sight (15:27). If they would, then the people could be assured that God would indeed be with them. But the people still wavered. The signs and wonders they had witnessed in Egypt were not enough. Though the people had experienced deliverance at the Sea of Reeds from the mighty army of Pharaoh, they still didn't seem to trust that YHWH, the Lord, was truly God and was going to take care of them. As noted earlier, God's sovereignty had to be demonstrated to two different audiences. One was Pharaoh, before whom God set numerous "signs and wonders." The other audience was the people of Israel. They too had witnessed what had happened in Egypt, but on the trip through the wilderness, God continued the divine effort to convince the skeptical.

We're Hungry! When Can We Stop?

Water was certainly the first priority, but food was also a matter of great concern. After the people had been on the move for about a month and a half, with supplies diminishing, they again began to complain to Moses and Aaron about their hunger (16:1–2). In that moment, the people remembered with longing the fish and vegetables they had had while they were still in Egypt. In their memory, there seemed to have been an abundance of food quite unlike what they were presently experiencing. Of course, they seemed to forget the backbreaking, spirit-killing slavery they also had had to endure, but that is the way it often is. Present needs often distort one's memory and can become a dominating force in one's life. The people turned their anxiety and frustration against Moses and Aaron, charging them with intentionally leading them out into the wilderness "to kill the whole assembly with hunger" (16:3).

Moses made an immediate reply. He challenged the people to consider what they were doing. They were griping to Moses, but their real problem lay somewhere else. Their actual complaint was against God and God's providential care. They were in effect asking, "Why isn't God taking care of us the way God should be doing?" So Moses told them, "In the evening you shall know that it was the LORD who brought you out of the land of Egypt, and in the morning you shall see the glory of the LORD, because he has heard your complaining" (16:6–7). God was about to meet their physical (and spiritual) needs once more in a dramatic manner. They were soon to have ample meat and bread to eat and plenty to ponder.

A double "miracle" was the divine response. In the evening, a vast number of quail flew into the camp (16:13). Some modern commentators have explained this phenomenon as a natural occurrence. In that area, birds have been blown off their normal migratory paths by strong winds. This might have been what the wanderers experienced. From the standpoint of the narrator, however, this was totally the work of God and in the category of what we moderns would call a miracle.

There was an equally surprising gift awaiting the people in the morning. The ground was covered with a layer of dew that, as it lifted, left behind a "fine flaky substance" unlike anything the people had thus far experienced (16:13–14). It was edible and breadlike, and since the people did not know what it was, they called it *manna*, which in Hebrew means, "What is it?" (16:15). Again, some modern commentators try to explain the manna as a natural occurrence. They note that certain insects in that region at different times of the year leave a deposit on the bushes and ground that is edible. This may have been what the Israelites encountered. The people themselves, however, did not know what to make of it. "[It] was like coriander seed, white, and the taste of it was like wafers made with honey" (16:31). This providential gift that fed the people throughout their many years of wandering was long remembered (16:33–35).

A Lesson in Listening and Following

The manna not only supplied a need for food, but it also was a test of the people's willingness to follow instructions and believe in God's commitment to them. God wanted to test the people—to check them out, so to speak (16:4). Moses was told to tell the people that they were to gather only enough manna each day for that day's need (16:4, 16). On the sixth day, they were to gather a supply for two days because the manna would not be provided on the seventh, or Sabbath, day (16:5, 22–26). The instructions were clear, but some of the people did not follow them. Some were greedy. They gathered more than they needed for one day, but to their dismay, the extra manna went bad during the night. Some were lazy and did not gather enough. Nonetheless, their daily needs were met (16:16–21). The petition in the Lord's Prayer to "give us this day our daily bread" is given a certain substance in light of the manna provision.

The main point of this account is clear: listen and obey. In response to the complaints of the Israelites, God provided liberally to address their problems. It was not wrong for them to make their needs known. They might have done it differently, though; they didn't really need to complain. Nonetheless, declaring legitimate needs before God is appropriate. Their request was heard, and they were given explicit instructions about how they were to act to benefit from God's gracious care. Their responsibility was to listen to what Moses told them and to follow those instructions. In Hebrew, the term we translate as "listen" can equally well be translated as "obey." The point is that if one actually listens to instructions, then one will understand and do what is expected. The people were expected to do as they were told in order to receive the provisions God was going to supply.

The report of the people's readiness to meet God's test is mixed. Apparently most of the people did as they were instructed, gathering the manna day by day in amounts sufficient for the day. Others, as already noted, did not demonstrate that they had listened because they did not obey. They tried to get more than their fair share of the manna and to hoard it, particularly on the sixth day. The Lord, in exasperation, said to Moses: "How long will you refuse to keep my commandments and instructions?" (16:28). God wanted the people's obedience, but it should be noted that this was not a prerequisite for receiving divine grace. God had already delivered the people. God had already demonstrated divine graciousness. This was not some sort of legalism required to win divine approval. This was simply what God knew was necessary for the people if they were to live in freedom. They needed to trust in God and act appropriately in that trust.

A Detour: Enmity with the Amalekites

While the Israelites were encamped at Rephidim, they were attacked by the Amalekites (17:8). Not much is known about the Amalekites. They seem to have been a seminomadic people living in the northern area of the Sinai Peninsula overlapping the area occupied by the Midianites. In earlier times they were found in the area southwest of the Dead Sea (see Gen. 14:7). One line of tradition identifies one of Esau's sons as Amalek, who became the progenitor of a clan that may have merged with the previously mentioned group of Amalekites (see Gen. 36:12, 16).

Why the Amalekites chose to fight with the Israelites is not clear. It may have been a territorial issue, the perceived threat to water and grazing rights. It may have been simply the need to demonstrate superiority, a kind of "male thing." Whatever the reason for the hostilities, Moses promptly assigned Joshua as leader of a group to fight with the Amalekites. (At this point in the narrative Joshua is a complete unknown. He has not figured in the story at all up to this point, and he is not introduced. Some commentators think that this story is out of place here and should be connected with the stories found in the book of Joshua.) On the following day, Moses, with Aaron and Hur, another leader of Israel, ascended a hill overlooking the battleground (17:9). Whenever Moses held up his hand, Joshua and his warriors prevailed, but the advantage was lost when Moses lowered his hand. To ensure Joshua's victory, Aaron and Hur propped Moses up with a stone and held his hands high (17:10–13).

After this engagement with the Amalekites, Moses was instructed to write down a somber word about their future: "I [God] will utterly blot out the remembrance of Amalek from under heaven" (17:14; see also Num. 24:20 and Deut. 25:17–19). Because of this utterance, the Amalekites became symbols of the enemies of Israel and of God. Much later in history, in the book of Esther, the major enemy of Esther's people was Haman, an Agagite, and thus, an Amalekite (see Esth. 3:1). Haman eventually was undone, and the festival of Purim was established as a reminder of the evil that Israel has at times had to face. Haman's wickedness has been memorialized in the continuing celebration of the Jewish festival of Purim with many comic representations being developed of the vicious Amalekites.

What is the point of this brief narrative that seems to come out of nowhere and then is dropped? First, it underscores the fact that in the Bible, God's salvation is often described in military terms. This continues in the New Testament when military language is used to speak of God's "war" with spiritual enemies. Second, this brief account is a reminder that Israel's life was in every way dependent on God. Without divine guidance and protection, Israel would never have come into being. God is dramatically claiming Israel as God's people. Israel will eventually reciprocate and accept YHWH as their God.

The Appearance of Jethro

The narrative continues with the unexpected, but quite welcome, arrival of Jethro and Moses' family: his wife Zipporah (Jethro's daughter) and their sons Gershom and Eliezer (18:2–4, 6). Jethro, known in the tradition also as Reuel (2:18; but see also Num. 10:29), was the Midianite (in Judg. 4:11 he is called a Kenite) whom Moses first met when he fled from Egypt (see 2:15–22). He was clearly a man of some wealth and served his people as both a leader and a priest (3:1). Jethro had heard of the great events surrounding Israel's departure from Egypt. Thus, he came out into the wilderness to meet Moses, who was encamped at the "mountain of God" and was greeted warmly (18:5, 7).

Moses reiterated all that had happened to him and to his people since he had left Jethro to return to Egypt (18:8). Jethro was greatly pleased to hear the story of God's deliverance of Israel from the hands of Pharaoh and the Egyptians (18:9–10). For Jethro, the story of Israel's rescue from the arrogance of the Egyptians was clear evidence of YHWH's superiority over all other gods (18:11). Then, acting in his capacity as priest, Jethro made "sacrifices to God," inviting Aaron and all the elders of Israel to share in the sacrificial meal (18:12).

This is startling in two ways. First, a non-Israelite priest openly worships the God of the exodus and is accepted by Israel's leaders. God was clearly envisioned by the narrator as more than simply a tribal deity. Others outside Israel could and did worship YHWH. Second, Jethro's faith was based on the accounts of others. He had not witnessed the signs and wonders performed by God in Egypt. He had not been present at Israel's deliverance at the Sea of Reeds. He raised his praise based on the witness of others and thus began a long line of people who would celebrate God's salvation secondhand, so to speak.

We need to pause again in our story. This event underscores the fact that history does not clearly reveal Israel's origins. There was a company of people that others called "Hebrews" living in Egypt. These Hebrews understood themselves as the offspring of Jacob, whose name had been changed to Israel (see Gen. 32:28). But they left Egypt with a "mixed crowd" (12:38) that apparently included many non-Hebrews. They then were led in worship by a Midianite (possibly Kenite) priest. Exactly who are these people? Later reflection will present them as a single folk who passed through the wilderness in an almost pristine manner. But that hardly seems likely. Far more likely is the view that understands "Israel" as a later theological construct given as the name for a wide mix of peoples who came together at various times convinced that YHWH had in various ways intervened in their lives for good. These were human beings that God met in their humanity and from which God fashioned a people.

The Guidance of Jethro

Before Jethro departed from the story he had one other major contribution to make. He observed his son-in-law being worked to death. Moses was expected to adjudicate every dispute among the people. They came to him from morning until night asking him to settle their differences. Moses explained that he had tried to teach them the "statutes and instructions of God," but they still wanted Moses to make all the decisions (18:13–15).

Jethro rightly pointed out the futility of this practice. Moses did not have enough time or energy to deal with every case brought before him (18:17–18). It was Moses' responsibility to intercede before God on behalf of the people and to teach them God's expectations, "the way they are to go and the things they are to do" (18:19–20). The actual day-by-day work had to be divided up, however. Jethro told Moses to choose men "who fear God, are trustworthy, and hate dishonest gain." They in turn were to preside over various groups organized in terms of the degree of seriousness of the problems presented. The lesser issues they were to decide, bringing only the really important issues to Moses (18:21–22). In other words, Moses needed to develop an effective committee system to spread the work around. Moses took Jethro's advice to heart and organized the people accordingly (18:24–26).

Thus, in the midst of this account about mysterious and miraculous events, there is a note of pragmatic, down-to-earth problem solving. The division of labor suggested by Jethro was an important contribution to the governing of the community. It was an obvious thing to do—after someone pointed it out! From the Bible's point of view, there should be no surprise when humans solve problems. Many times God does not do it for us. Rather, God enables us to glimpse God's way and to develop appropriate actions on our own. Either way, we humans are the beneficiaries of God's wisdom.

Conclusion

The story of Israel's journey from Egypt to the mountain of God was marked by a number of memorable events. The basic human needs of water and food were met by miraculous gifts. Quail and manna—what a feast! The people were successful in military conflict. Moses was guided in priestly and judicial matters by Jethro, who appears unexpectedly and then departs. Through it all, God is recognized as the Lord of all gods. The Israelites had asked the question "Is the LORD among us or not?" That was the fundamental issue for the people and the one that God sought to resolve. Through the various experiences the people underwent, they were being shaped to become the covenant people God wanted them to be. They were almost ready for the great transforming events soon to take place at Sinai.

Chapter Five

Sinai and God's Covenant

A Study of Exodus 19:1–21:11; 24:1–18

Thus far in Exodus we have explored the great escape, God's deliverance of Israel out of the bondage of Egypt. The signs and wonders that wrought the discomfort and dismay of the Egyptian people eventually confounded Pharaoh as well. The safe passage through the Sea of Reeds and the destruction of Pharaoh's army culminated with Israel's departure from Egypt. This is the first defining event in Israel's story.

Now we turn to the second extraordinary account of the formation of Israel as God's covenant people. The events take place on a mountain somewhere to the east of Egypt that is known both as Horeb and as Sinai. This is remembered in the tradition as the most foundational revelation of God to Israel and the point at which Israel and God become inextricably bound to one another.

The Scene Is Set

The Israelites encamped at the foot of Mount Sinai "on the third new moon" after they left Egypt (19:1–2). As already noted, the exact whereabouts of Sinai

---

are debated, but it was somewhere in the midst of a great wilderness and not easily reached. The people had traveled for several months before they reached it. They probably did not know why Moses had led them to this remote place, but they soon learned.

After they had settled down, Moses "went up to God," which presumably means that he ascended the mountain (19:3). God told him what to say to the people about the significance of what would soon happen. The Israelites were to be reminded that they had witnessed what God had done to the Egyptians. On God's own initiative, God had plucked the Israelites out of Egypt as "on eagles' wings" and had brought them safely to Sinai (19:4). Now they were to become God's "treasured possession out of all the peoples."

All people belong to God because the whole earth is God's, but Israel was to be special (19:5). There was one stipulation. Israel had to obey God's voice and keep God's covenant" (19:5). The terms used to describe Israel are interesting. Israel was to be for God "a priestly kingdom and a holy nation" (19:6). These terms emphasized both the civil and the religious aspects of Israel's calling: Israel was to be a "kingdom" and a "nation"—sociopolitical language. At the same time, the Israelites were to be "priests" in the service of God and "holy"—religious language. When Moses declared God's intention and condition, the people responded, "Everything that the LORD has spoken we will do" (19:8). The tension between Israel's special designation as "holy" while at the same time being very much a part of the real world of power and politics can be seen throughout the history that followed.

Getting the People Ready

Moses spent the next several days getting the people ready for their encounter with God. Nothing was to be left to chance. The people had to be "consecrated," set apart. The ordinary had to be made special. Moses had the people wash their clothes (19:10, 14). Ritual washing has long been a means of acknowledging the need to leave the old behind for the new that is to come. Not only were the people to prepare by washing their garments, but they were also told not to ascend or even touch the mountain. Nor were their animals permitted to touch the mountain. Any person or animal that came into contact with the area set apart was to be put to death by being stoned or shot with arrows. No one was to touch these people or animals because they would have become contaminated by touching the forbidden mountain (19:12–13). One further warning was made. The men were to have no contact with the women (19:15). No reason for this is given. God was going to "come down upon Mount Sinai" in the "sight of all the people." They had to be ready, for this presented a very real danger as well as an enormous blessing.

The issue of consecration seems strange to many today. Few have a strong sense of what "holiness" means or why being in the presence of God might seem dangerous. The otherness of God is a foreign idea among those who tend to view God as a "buddy" or "friend," if indeed they think of God at all. To the ancients, the divine was mysterious and somewhat threatening, and thus it was important to prepare properly before entering the sanctuary. About as near as most come to any such notion today is the desire by some to dress nicely when they go to church. The Israelites, on the other hand, were about to have a mountaintop experience so totally different from what we tend to think of when we hear that term and they would never be the same afterward. They were about to meet the Holy One.

The Appearance of God

"On the morning of the third day there was thunder and lightening, as well as a thick cloud on the mountain, and a blast of a trumpet so loud that all the people who were in the camp trembled" (19:16). So begins the description of the divine descent to Mount Sinai. An appearance of God such as this is called a theophany. Some suggest that an erupting volcano offers the best notion of what is being described. The mountain smoked and violently shook (19:18). There was the piercing blast of a ram's horn (Hebrew: *shophar*) that grew louder and louder to the point of becoming deafening. When Moses spoke to God, thunderous responses came back in answer (19:19). The people were warned once again not to approach the mountain lest they perish. Even the priests had to be especially careful (19:21–22). The mountain was to be kept holy, with nothing profane allowed on it. If these instructions were violated, God might well break out against the offenders with the direst of consequences (19:23). The only exceptions were for Moses and Aaron, who were allowed to approach God on the holy mountain (19:24).

The words of the narrator are not sufficient to describe the appearance of God. God's presence was mystifying, terrifying, fascinating, and indescribable. For many moderns the term "God" has become so domesticated that this narrative is unintelligible and hardly believable. Moderns want to control God and enjoy the divine on their own terms. YHWH will have nothing of such an understanding. God comes on God's own terms, when, where, and in whatever form God chooses. For Elijah, centuries later, it was in the "sound of sheer silence" (1 Kgs. 19:11–13). For Isaiah, it was centered on the holy of holies in the temple, from which streamed forth in the midst of smoke the very hem of God's royal garment (Isa. 6:1). For Ezekiel, it was in a vision of a chariot throne surrounded by blazing light and attended by angelic figures (Ezek. 1:4–28). YHWH will not be tamed or controlled. God is God, and God's ways are not the ways of humans.

God's Covenant with Israel

The aim of God's appearance on Mount Sinai was to establish a covenant with Israel (19:5). A covenant is somewhat like a contract or marriage agreement. It is public and binds the covenanting parties in a mutually agreed-on relationship. There were several types of covenants in antiquity. Those in Genesis on which the relationship with Abraham, Isaac, and Jacob/Israel was based were promissory covenants, which had no stipulations, just God's promise (Gen. 15:5; 17:7–8; 26:24; 28:13–14). The covenant in Exodus, in contrast, is a covenant of obligation. We know the most about this form of covenant from the literary remains of two groups in antiquity: the Hittites (in the area of modern Turkey) of the fourteenth century BCE and the Assyrians (in the area of modern Iraq) of the seventh century BCE.

These covenants are in effect international treaties. They are called suzerainty treaties and involve overlords (the suzerains) imposing a "peace" treaty on conquered underlings (the vassals). In the language of these covenants, the overlords are called "father" and the underlings are called "sons." A suzerainty treaty generally has a section that recalls the history of the prior relationship between the involved parties, especially emphasizing the way the suzerain rescued the vassal from attacks by hostile neighbors or from other difficulties. Then the parties agree to be in covenant with one another. This involves a pledge on the part of the more powerful to protect and care for the less powerful. In turn, the less powerful agrees to carry out a number of stipulations that involve everything from paying annual tribute to coming to the aid of the suzerain or other vassals of the suzerain as directed.

From archaeological evidence we know that these treaties were widely used in the fourteenth and seventh centuries BCE, but it is unclear if they were used in other periods. Thus, though it cannot be proved absolutely, it seems possible that the writers of Exodus (and especially Deuteronomy) had suzerainty treaties or covenants in mind when they sought to describe the way God engaged Israel in covenant. This worldly political model provided a workable metaphor for God's covenant with Israel. There was the historical memory of God's past relationships with the forebears in the book of Genesis underscored by the memory of the events that brought Israel out of Egypt and to the holy mountain (Exod. 3–18). As a culmination of the covenanting between God and Israel, a whole set of stipulations was fashioned for Israel's assurance and guidance. God was committed to the care and protection of Israel, and Israel was bound to live in God's way. Obedience on the part of Israel (the vassal) was required, but this did not earn the covenant; it simply confirmed it and testified to it. Only God (the suzerain) could initiate and enact the covenantal agreement; Israel had the freedom and responsibility to accept or reject it.

Covenant Stipulations: The Ten Words

The Ten Commandments—or as they are known in Hebrew, the Ten Words—are the most well known of the biblical covenant stipulations. They are found in two versions (Exod. 20:1–17 and Deut. 5:6–21), which, while being essentially the same, have several differences. They were given to Moses from the dense cloud that covered the top of Mount Sinai upon which God's glory had settled (19:9, 16; 24:16–17). Moses alone entered the cloud (20:21; 24:18). He eventually came forth with two stone tablets on which the Ten Words had been inscribed by the very "finger of God" (24:12; 31:18; 32:15–16). These commandments provide a basic summary of the way God expected Israel to live as the covenant partner God had selected.

These commandments are what scholars call apodictic laws. They are absolute and universal. "You shall not . . ." is the language used to express these apodictic commands. They stand in contrast to other statutes and ordinances that are written in what is called casuistic form: if such and such happens, then you shall do such and such.

The first four of the Ten Commandments deal with the matter of worship (20:1–11). Immediately following the brief historical reminder of God's saving work with Israel (20:2), the people are instructed to have no other god than YHWH. They are to make no idols of any type but are to worship only God. The word translated "worship" also can be translated "serve." It is the same word used to describe Israel's "service" before Pharaoh. God is to be their divine master, rather than a human such as Pharaoh. They are to worship or serve YHWH alone (20:3–5). They are reminded that God is zealous, punishing wrongdoers but also showing steadfast love to those who keep the divine instructions (20:5–7). The longest of the four initial commandments deals with honoring the Sabbath day in remembrance of God's rest after the creation of the world (20:8–11). In Deuteronomy, the observance of a day of rest is supported on the basis that the people had once been enslaved and knew what a blessing rest can be (Deut. 5:15).

The remaining six commandments deal with the relationships the Israelites were to have with one another. They were to honor and care for their aging parents (20:12). Murder, adultery, stealing, false witness, and coveting were forbidden (20:13–17). It is noteworthy that there are a number of stipulations later in the text about various forms of thievery and the appropriate punishment to be meted out (see 22:1–4). Thus, the commandment against "stealing" may well have been originally understood as forbidding "kidnapping," which was a capital offense (20:15; see 21:16 and Deut. 24:7). In many ways, these commandments are a matter of common sense. A community cannot long thrive if such behavior goes unchecked. They are echoed in the legal codes of many different people across the centuries. Nonetheless, they are uttered here with divine authority. These are covenant stipulations, the breaking of which will bring dire consequences.

Covenant Stipulations: The Covenant Code

Another collection of statutes and ordinances followed the Ten Commandments (20:22–23:19). Scholars call this material the Covenant Code or the Book of the Covenant (24:7). It is a mixed group of instructions that generally take a casuistic form. A basic rule is stated, but then exceptions are recognized and alternative action is given. For instance, the commandment against the making of idols is reiterated (20:23) but then expanded to include instruction about sacrifice and the sufficiency of earthen altars (20:24). But—and here comes the casuistry—if an altar of stone is constructed, then certain stipulations are to be followed (20:25–26).

Another example concerns an ordinance dealing with Hebrew slaves. Hebrews were not to enslave one another. Therefore, should a Hebrew become indentured to another Hebrew, then that slave was to be released after six years of service (21:2). If that slave was single when he was acquired, however, he was to go out single even if he had married while he was serving as slave (21:3). The slave would have to leave behind his wife and any children (21:4). But, again, if the slave chose not to leave his family behind, that slave then could declare his desire to remain with the one whom he served and become a slave for life (21:5–6).

The Covenant Code contains rulings about a variety of topics, from property (21:28–36) to appropriate restitution to be made in various circumstances (22:1–15). Some of the material seems to put some of the Ten Words into a different but understandable form (21:12–27). These stipulations are expanded greatly in the book of Leviticus. It is noteworthy that many of the laws found in the Covenant Code assume that Israel is an agricultural people living a settled life.

While the Ten Words can equally apply to sedentary as well as semi-nomadic groups, the ordinances preserved in the Book of the Covenant generally deal with situations that arise among people who have settled down. These rules seem to be quite old, and they reflect life after Israel had entered Canaan, not while Israel was wandering in the wilderness. This is another witness to the complexity of the Bible's development. It was not simply written down all at one time in one place. The name of Moses and the authority of Moses are attached to all these stipulations, but they in fact seem to have developed over a long period of time and in a variety of different circumstances, many of them long after the time of Moses.

The Sealing of the Covenant

After Moses had received the Ten Words, he presented all the commandments and ordinances to the people. They in turn pledged to do all that the Lord had spoken (24:3). Moses then wrote down all the words, built an altar at the foot of Mount Sinai, and had twelve pillars erected to represent the twelve tribes of Israel (24:4). Numerous sacrifices were offered to the Lord, with half of the blood of the slain animals thrown on the altar (24:6). Moses again read the whole Book of the Covenant to the people. When they repeated their pledge to obey God's stipulations, Moses dashed the rest of the blood taken from the slain animals on the people, saying, "See the blood of the covenant that the LORD has made with you in accordance with all these words" (24:7–8).

There are two unusual features about this report. First, the importance of blood is not obvious to most moderns. In ancient Israel, the blood of sacrificial animals was to be drained before the sacrifice was offered to God. The blood was understood as the seat of life. It had power to cleanse and to cement relationships. To be sprinkled with blood was to be sanctified, set apart, enabled to participate in the holiness of the sacrifice. We may view the whole affair as messy and unnecessary, but for the Israelites it was a most important part of any sacrifice or making of a covenant.

Second, this sounds like the report of a ceremony that had been developed carefully and executed over a number of years. It doesn't sound like something that could have just happened on the spot out in the wilderness. The liturgy of reading the covenantal words and the response of the people sounds like something that was more rehearsed than the narrative would suggest. It seems quite possible that a ceremony developed after the people had entered Canaan was read back into the time of Moses.

An even more dramatic and unusual event is also described. Moses had been instructed to bring Aaron, Nadab, Abihu (two of Aaron's sons), and seventy of the elders of Israel to worship "at a distance" (24:1). Moses alone was to ascend to the summit of Mount Sinai (24:2). After the sprinkling of the blood, all those who had at first remained at a distance "went up" (24:9). Then—and this is the shocker—the text tells us that "they saw the God of Israel" (24:10)! Elsewhere the tradition insists that no one can see God and live (33:20), but that is not the report here.

Beyond that remarkable claim, two other things are noteworthy. First, though they saw God, there is no effort to describe God. There was "something like a pavement of sapphire stone, like the very heaven for clearness" (24:10; see Ezek. 1:4–28). God was there. They saw God. But there were no words capable of communicating what that really was like. The second astonishing note is that "God did not lay his hand on the chief men of the people of Israel; also they beheld God, and they ate and drank" (24:11). The covenant with its concrete obligations is ratified, so to speak, with a mystical meal shared in the presence of the holy, indescribable God.

Moses Enters the Cloud

The narrative we are considering concludes as improbably as it began. Moses again was instructed to come up to the mountaintop to receive tablets of stone on which God had written "the law and the commandment" (24:12). Joshua went part of the way, but the others remained behind (24:13–14). Moses approached the summit as the cloud that had covered the mountaintop from the Lord's first appearing covered it again (24:15; see also 19:16, 20). We are told that "the glory of the LORD settled on Mount Sinai" (24:16). The terminology in Hebrew indicates that God's visitation on the mountain was not permanent but was only for a brief, indefinite time. Further, it was not actually God who descended on the mountain, but the "glory of the LORD," a luminous light like "a devouring fire" (24:17). For the priestly tradition in Israel, God's glory (Hebrew: *kabod*) was the supreme symbol of divine presence. Later in the prophetic tradition, God's word (Hebrew: *dabar*) was to be put forward in challenge to the priestly claim. In this narrative, however, God's glory surrounded Moses as Moses entered the cloud, where he stayed for "forty days and forty nights"—a very long time to be in the presence of the Holy One (24:18).

Conclusion

This remarkable section of Exodus has preserved some spectacular accounts. From the departure into the wilderness with the unexpected provision of quail and manna to the covenant-sealing meal in the very presence of God, the story captures the wonder of God's care for Israel. God gives Israel commandments as a gracious guide for a full and productive life. The lack of trust displayed by Israel, however, which took the form of complaining against Moses, foreshadowed a tendency to disobedience on the part of the people that was repeated many times. Nonetheless, it was the mercy and compassion of God that prevailed.

Chapter Six

Rebellion and Forgiveness

A Study of Exodus 32:1–34:35

The capacity of humans to mess up seems limitless. Relationships with one another can unexpectedly turn sour because of an unguarded comment or unintended slight. Family members have been known to go for years without speaking to one another because of something done or undone. Sometimes the offending party does not even know what or how they hurt the feelings of the other. Once the deed is done, however, achieving reconciliation is extremely difficult.

Forgiveness is easy to talk about and difficult to do. To forgive someone does not mean that the offense is forgotten, but rather that the offender is given a second chance. People ask God for forgiveness all the time, but it is usually phrased in general, nonspecific language that suggests that the person asking does not actually believe there is any real need to be forgiven.

In the Exodus passages considered in this chapter, the reality of sin is clearly demonstrated. Equally vivid is the work of Moses as intercessor before God. Most dramatic, however, is God's willingness and ability to offer the offending people the second chance, a response humans too often refuse.

A Dramatic Breach of Covenant

After a long digression concerning the construction of a tabernacle and various ritual matters (25:1–31:17), the narrator returns to the story. The scene opens with the notice that Moses was still absent from the people. He had disappeared into the heavy cloud that rested on Mount Sinai. The people did not know where he was or whether he would return. They likewise were uncertain whether what had happened between them and God was real or only a dream. They wanted assurance of the presence of God, so they asked Aaron, "Make gods for us, who shall go before us" (32:1; see also 17:7). Aaron immediately complied.

The passage gives two versions of Aaron's complicity. In the first, Aaron receives gold offered by the people, melts it in a mold, and produces a golden calf (32:2–4). In the second, Aaron claims less responsibility for the outcome by saying that he simply threw the gold into the fire and out came the calf (32:24). At any rate, when the people saw the golden calf, they responded, "These are your gods, O Israel, who brought you up out of the land of Egypt" (32:4, 8). It is debated whether the golden calf was considered an actual representation of God—in Canaanite religion a bull is a symbol for the deity Baal—or whether the gold object was simply a pedestal on which the invisible God was enthroned. However it is interpreted, in the popular mind the presence of YHWH had been assured with a piece of metal! This was tantamount to a rebellion. The first three basic covenant stipulations, the first three commandments (20:3–5), had been violated.

God's reaction was strong and negative. God ordered Moses to return to the people immediately. So far as God was concerned, the people were Moses' people rather than God's people (32:7). Israel had been "quick to turn aside from the way" that God had commanded (32:8). They were "stiff-necked," and God was prepared to turn from them and work through Moses to "make a great nation." God expected the stipulations of the covenant to be kept. The people deserved severe punishment, and God was prepared for the divine wrath "to burn hot against them" and "consume them" (32:9–10).

The Intercession of Moses

Moses immediately stepped between God and the people. With the choice of the pronoun "your," the narrator makes clear, so far as Moses was concerned, that the people were still God's people (32:11). Moses appealed to God on two accounts. First, were God to destroy Israel at this point in their journey, then the Egyptians could claim that God had brought the people out into the wilderness for the express purpose of killing them, something that God certainly would not want the Egyptians to be able to claim (32:12). Second, Moses reminded God of the promises to Abraham, Isaac, and Jacob, and quoted from Genesis 15:5: "I will multiply your descendants like the stars of heaven, and all this land that I have promised I will give to your descendants, and they shall inherit it forever" (32:13). These promises were the reason God had determined to deliver Israel from Egypt in the first place (2:24; 6:5–8).

In response to this twofold appeal, "the LORD changed his mind about the disaster that he planned to bring on his people" (32:14). There is no argument about the justice of the divine punishment planned. The narrator considered it totally justified. The people had violated their covenantal obligations and deserved punishment. Some today seem to think it unfair for God to hold people to account, but the narrator of this passage does not. What is remarkable, however, and difficult for some to consider even as a possibility, is that God's mind was changed! Some theologians don't think that God should be allowed such freedom, and they describe God with words such as "immutable" and "unchangeable." But the Bible does not present God in that way. When it is appropriate to do so, God can and will change plans, particularly when the issue is to forgive or not to forgive.

When Moses reached the camp and saw the revelry of the people, he threw down the two tablets he had brought down from the summit, the two tables of God's commandments, breaking them to pieces (32:15–16, 19). He then destroyed the molten image and ground it to powder, which he sprinkled into water and made the people drink (32:20). Moses reprimanded Aaron, who in turn pled for Moses to protect him from the divine wrath (32:21–24). Aaron blamed the people (32:22), but the narrator suggests that Aaron was responsible for letting the people "run wild" (32:25). Moses instructed the sons of Levi (who had volunteered at Moses' invitation) to execute those most deeply involved (some three thousand) with no regard for whether they were relatives or friends (32:26–28). By their action, they demonstrated their worthiness for the "service of the LORD" (32:29). They would become the core priestly group who would attend to the service of God in the tabernacle.

After the disastrous confrontation and its deadly consequences, Moses addressed the people: "You have sinned a great sin. But now I will go up to the LORD; perhaps I can make atonement for your sin" (32:30). Even though they were guilty of a serious breach of the covenant, of making "gods of gold," Moses pled to God for divine forgiveness. In fact, he went so far as to put himself in jeopardy on behalf of the people. If God was unwilling to forgive their sin, then Moses wanted to be punished with them, telling God, "Blot me [Moses] out of the book that you have written" (32:31–32). God was not prepared to blot Moses out—Moses had not sinned against God—but reserved the right to punish later any and all who did sin against God (32:33–34).

On the Road Again

Though the people's relationship with God was still somewhat tenuous, the Lord ordered Moses and the people to leave Sinai/Horeb and head for the land promised to Abraham, Isaac, and Jacob (33:1). God intended for them to enter the land of "the Canaanites, the Amorites, the Hittites, the Perizzites, the Hivites, and the Jebusites"—a land "flowing with milk and honey" (33:2–3; see Gen. 15:18–21; Exod. 23:23; 34:11). God did not plan to go with them, however, for they were "stiff-necked" and would be destroyed by the divine presence (33:2–3). When the people learned that God would not go with them, they stripped themselves of all ornamentation and mourned (33:4, 6). Then they waited to see if God would reconsider (33:5).

In the midst of this tense account, a detour is taken. We learn of a "tent of meeting" that existed before the tabernacle, which was soon to be constructed. This tent was set up outside the boundaries of the camp because it was the sanctuary where people went to seek the presence of the holy God (33:7; see also 25:8–9). When Moses went out to the tent of meeting and entered it, the pillar of cloud symbolizing the presence of God "would descend and stand at the entrance of the tent" (33:8–9; see also 13:21–22; 14:19). When the people saw the pillar of cloud, they bowed down to the Lord (33:10). God maintained connection with the people through Moses, with whom God spoke "face to face, as one speaks to a friend" (33:11). This remarkable vignette is matter-of-factly reported and placed in the midst of a drama centering on the question of whether God's continuing presence will be with Israel or not. Here there seems to be no question, but in the verses preceding and following, the matter is very much up in the air.

The narrative continues with Moses posing this very question to God. Moses had been instructed to bring the people up, but God had as yet not made clear whether God was going to be with Moses during the journey. Moses again reminded God that Israel was God's people and deserved to know God's intentions (33:12–13). At this point, God assured Moses that the divine presence would go with them (33:15). But Moses was not through with the matter: "If your presence will not go, do not carry us up from here. For how shall it be known that I have found favor in your sight, I and your people, unless you go with us?" (33:15–16). Moses wanted more than God's assurance; Moses wanted to see God's glory (Hebrew: *kabod*), the luminescence of the very presence of the divine (33:18).

Moses was not to see God's glory, for no one was allowed to see God's face and live (33:20; but see 24:1–11). Rather, as confirmation that God would indeed go with Moses and the people, God said to Moses, "I will make all my goodness pass before you, and will proclaim before you the name, 'The LORD'; and I will be gracious to whom I will be gracious, and will show mercy on whom I will show mercy" (33:19). Then God placed Moses in "a cleft of the rock" and with a hand covered him so that he saw only the back of God (33:22).

The Proclamation of God's Name

This was certainly a dramatic way to give Moses assurance of the divine presence, but something more astounding was to follow. Moses was instructed to fashion two new tablets of stone so that God could once again inscribe the covenantal stipulations on them (34:1). He was to ascend by himself to the top of Sinai, where God would meet him. There he would receive commandments to replace those that he had earlier smashed to pieces (34:2–4).

At this point in the text, something truly extraordinary occurs. In a brief poetic utterance, the character of God is sketched in unforgettable language (34:6–7). This beautiful, succinct description of God is repeated in whole or in part in at least ten other passages in the Old Testament (Num. 14:18; 2 Chron. 30:9; Neh. 9:17; Ps. 86:15; 103:8; 145:8; Jer. 32:18; Joel 2:13; Jonah 4:2; and Nahum 1:3). This is neither a recitation of divine attributes nor an exploration of the essence of God as an exercise of philosophical reflection on the divine being. Rather, it is a testimony to the way God engages humankind in relationship. It is a hymn to the wonder of God, whose presence will accompany Moses and the people wherever they go.

What do we learn about God, whose name, YHWH, was twice repeated as God passed before Moses (34:6a)? God is merciful (Hebrew: *rachum*). This term is derived from the Hebrew word for "womb" (*rechem*) and conveys the notion of a motherlike love and devotion to her child. God's mercy is as long lasting as a mother's love. God is also gracious (Hebrew: *hannun*), granting to humans totally unmerited favor (such as Moses: 33:12, 16–17). Beyond anything that warrants such action, God is nonetheless gracious and merciful to whomever God chooses (33:19). What's more, this is done by one who is "slow to anger" (33:6)—literally in Hebrew, by one "whose nose is long." Anger is expressed with the metaphor of a flared, expanded nose—a "hot nose." But the opposite, as an expression of patience, one is said to have a relaxed, smooth, "long nose," thus being "slow to anger."

God is also described as "abounding in steadfast love and faithfulness" (34:6b). "Steadfast love" is a frequent translation for the Hebrew term *chesed*, which is a covenantal term. It can also be rendered as "devoted love" or "loyalty." When one has *chesed*, one will go to any length to maintain a relationship, even if one's actions are not reciprocated. In another part of the Bible, a young David is being pursued by his king, Saul, who wants to kill him. David has the perfect opportunity to slay Saul, knowing that no one would fault him. But he does not. Why? Because he is King Saul's subject, and *chesed* requires his continued allegiance (1 Sam. 24:1–22). The term "steadfast love" often is used in parallel with the term translated "faithfulness" (Hebrew: *'emet*), which denotes a firm constancy and reliability.

God keeps *chesed* for a very long time—indeed, for the "thousandth generation" (Exod. 33:7a). This devoted loyalty on the part of God for the covenant means that God is willing to forgive, to "lift up" (Hebrew: *nasa'*), and thus to remove "iniquity and transgression and sin"—in other words, to remove every form of covenantal violation from those who have sinned. This is very good news! But at the same time, and in seeming contradiction to the assurance of forgiveness, God will punish offenders even to the "third and fourth generation" (33:7b). The point is that "iniquity, transgression, and sin" are serious matters that cannot simply be wished away or swept under the proverbial rug. God is able to deal appropriately with wrongdoers while nonetheless showing loyalty and forgiveness to vast multitudes for a very long time. When punishment is forthcoming, it is directed at the wrongdoers and is appropriate to their misdeeds. The language about the "third and fourth generation" underscores the collective nature of wrongdoing—in ancient Israel, three or four generations usually occupied the same living space—and was intended as a counter to an open-ended, endless kind of curse that was sometimes attributed to deities.

This beautiful expression of the character of God's relationship with Israel may well have been used in ritual settings for generations. What should be remembered in this literary setting is that it comes in response to the dramatic transgression involving the casting of the bull image recounted in chapter 32. Some were punished at that point (32:28), but all the people were not blotted out, though they might well have deserved it in light of their disobedience. All Moses could do in response to this proclamation of the divine name was to bow in worship. He then acknowledged that the people were indeed stiff-necked and begged God to once again demonstrate the amazing mercy, grace, patience, steadfast love, and faithfulness of which God spoke and to forgo the visitation of punishment on the people even though they deserved it (34:8–9).

The Covenant Renewed

God's response to Moses' prayer was as gracious as Moses had hoped. God once again entered into covenant with Israel, vowing to demonstrate the divine commitment through "marvels, such as have not been performed in all the earth or in any nation," so that all the peoples might see the wondrous work of God (34:10). The exact nature of these "marvels" is not spelled out, but the Hebrew word (*pela'*) is the same as that translated "wonder" in reference to God's dealings with the Egyptians (see 3:20; 15:11). God was to do "an awesome thing" with Israel, and all would recognize God's special relationship with Israel (34:10).

As a result of this covenant, God was going to make a place for Israel in the area occupied by "the Amorites, the Canaanites, the Hittites, the Perizzites, the Hivites, and the Jebusites"—namely, the hill country of what came to be called Palestine (34:11). Israel was not to enter into any covenants with the peoples of that territory lest they and their culture, particularly their religious practices, "become a snare" (34:11–13). To read between the lines: No more golden calves!

What follows is a set of commandments that deal primarily with various ritual practices suited mainly for life within the agricultural setting of Canaan. Instructions concerning the festivals of unleavened bread, weeks, first fruits, and ingathering (34:18, 22) and the Sabbath (34:21) are given. Guidance for the sacrifices of redemption of the firstborn and firstfruits is offered (34:19–20, 25–26). How old these commandments are is impossible to determine. They appear to have been sufficiently authoritative that they could be included as stipulations of the covenant with the Lord. They did not replace the Ten Commandments; nonetheless, they were worthy of preservation at a significant point in Israel's story.

The Ongoing Relationship of Moses with God

The next section of the narrative concludes in a somewhat strange manner. There are two aspects of the account that catch the reader's attention. First, God and Moses continued to have contact long after Moses came down from Mount Sinai. That Moses had been in the presence of God was evident to all because the skin of his face shone (34:29, 35). Moses adopted the custom of wearing a veil to cover his face when he walked among the people, apparently to spare them discomfort. When he entered the tent of meeting, he would remove the veil; when he came out, he would cover himself again (34:33–35). The exact cause of this unusual occurrence is not explained. The most obvious reason might be that the bright glow of God's "glory" was transferred in part to Moses' face, but we are not told why this happened.

What is important to note is that this was clearly a sign of divine presence. That had been the issue for Moses and the people from the start of their excursion with God. Moses had been assured before he ever confronted Pharaoh that God would be with him (3:12; 4:12). In the wilderness, the people had questioned whether God was in their midst (17:7). After the debacle of the golden calf, Moses was concerned whether God's presence would continue with the Israelites, and God reassured him (32:14). Moses had prayed for God's presence after receiving the proclamation of God's name (34:9). Moses' glowing, shining face was the eloquent sign for all to see of God's continuing presence.

The second aspect of this account worth special consideration is the emphasis on the spoken word. Not much is said in the Bible about the appearance of God. The more important issue is what God says. God talked with Moses (34:29, 32, 34–35), and when that happened, Moses' face would glow. Equally important, Moses talked with the leaders of the people (34:31) and with the people as a whole (34:32–34). Moses "gave them [the people] in commandment all that the LORD had spoken with him on Mount Sinai" (34:32). As intercessor for the people before God and as spokesman for God before the people, there was no one equal to Moses. God was indeed with him, giving him significant words to provide substance to his shining face. In the last verses of the Pentateuch (the first five books of the Bible, called the Torah in Jewish tradition), in the book of Deuteronomy, we read these words about Moses: "Never since has there arisen a prophet in Israel like Moses, whom the LORD knew face to face" (Deut. 34:10).

Conclusion

The account we have considered is one of the most important in Exodus and in the Bible. Because of the overt disregard of the Ten Words by God's covenant partner Israel, the relationship between God and Israel was placed in jeopardy. By worshiping a golden idol, Israel totally violated the promise to live within the covenant commitment. Moses desperately and bravely pled before the Lord for forgiveness. This was granted and was confirmed by the beautiful affirmation that God is to be understood as "merciful and gracious, slow to anger, and abounding in steadfast love and faithfulness." God gave Moses and the people assurance that the divine presence would be in their midst. It is this word of assurance that motivated the construction of the tabernacle, which is the subject of the next chapter.

Chapter Seven

The Tabernacle
and God's Presence

A Study of Exodus 25:1–40; 26:30–37; 39:32–43;
40:16–38

A place of worship is important for many people. They want the familiarity of a particular place and a special setting. They construct all sorts of buildings, from simple, one-room country churches to magnificent cathedrals in their efforts to meet what they consider a basic requirement for religious expression. In most instances, these places of worship are situated on property specially chosen for the purpose; in other words, they are anchored to a piece of real estate. If the occasion arises that requires the removal or relocating of a church, there is often great commotion within the congregation.

In antiquity, there were also designated places of worship, some large, some small. Some were household shrines. Some were simple altars set amid a grove of trees or on a hill. Some were monumental buildings that could accommodate a very large assembly. But there was one other type that is much less common in modern society: the movable shrine. Such shrines were used by nomadic groups and were carried on a wagon or an animal and then erected when a resting place was reached. The tabernacle that is at the center of this chapter was such a movable shrine.

A Word about the Narrative Setting

We have followed the narrative of Israel's rescue and departure from Egypt fairly closely. The only dramatic departure from the story line occurred in chapter 6, which centered on Exodus 32–34 after the preceding material (25:1–31:17) had been skipped. There was a purpose for that, and it has to do with the way the narrator structured the traditions preserved in Exodus.

Chapters 25–31 describe planning for constructing and equipping the tabernacle. Chapters 35–40 describe the carrying out of the plans and the erecting of the holy shrine. Logically, the chapters should have been continuous, with no break in between. But the narrator strategically placed the episode concerning Israel's sinful attachment to a graven image (chaps. 32–34) right at the center of the narrative for dramatic effect. In the midst of providing a place where God might meet with the people in their worship, grievous sin was committed. The ongoing testing of divine patience—by Israel and down to people in modern times—is expressed well by the arrangement of the material that we now have. That is not to be forgotten. Nonetheless, for the sake of convenience, this Exodus study concludes by focusing on the construction and outfitting of the tabernacle in one chapter.

The Mode of Divine Presence

How God's presence was to abide with humans was a matter of great debate during the course of Israel's history. One line of thought—basically associated with priestly circles—held that God dwelled (Hebrew: *yashav*) in Israel's midst. After the temple of Solomon had been constructed in Jerusalem, some believed that God dwelled there, that God had taken up permanent residence in that particular place. The priestly circles believed that God's glory (*kabod*) "dwelled" in the temple of Solomon. Others, especially those connected with the prophetic circles, insisted that God never "dwelled" with the people but only "tented" (*shakan*) with them. God did not take up permanent residence but only settled temporarily with them. On the basis of the root *shakan* ("to tent"), the English term "tabernacle" has been developed. Thus, to say that God "tabernacled" with the people was to emphasize the impermanence of God's presence. The prophetic circles thought further that only God's "name" actually tabernacled in the temple.

This is the point that is at stake in Exodus 25:1–9. A freewill offering was called for "from all whose hearts prompt them to give" (25:2). Presumably the offering was to come from the "gifts" that the Israelites had received from their Egyptian neighbors when they departed Egypt (3:21–22; 12:35–36). The offering was intended to provide the special materials—all manner of precious metals and stones, fine cloth and animal skins, special wood and oils—that would be required for doing what God wanted them to do (25:3–7).

What did God desire them to do? God told Moses to have the people make a sanctuary (Hebrew: *miqdash*), a holy place where God might, according to the NRSV, "dwell," but the Hebrew should be read as "tabernacle" (25:8). Further, a "tabernacle" (the noun *mishkan* from the verb *shakan*) was to be constructed for the divine presence (25:9). The choice of language was important. There was no intention of minimizing the significance of God's aim to dwell with the people as they moved away from Sinai. Nonetheless, it was important to make clear that this was not a permanent, unalterable commitment on the part of God. YHWH was always free to go or come or stay as YHWH chose.

God declared a commitment to accompany Moses and the people through the wilderness (25:8). Thus, it was only proper for them to construct an appropriate sanctuary in which God could choose to dwell as long as God desired. What's more, all was to be constructed according to an explicit, detailed pattern that God showed to Moses (25:9). Remember that this account is located in the narrative before the golden calf episode.

The Special Furnishings for the Tabernacle

While numerous articles were placed in the tabernacle when it was completed, there were four special pieces of furniture that were to be built and situated in particular places in the shrine. The first was a rectangular box or chest (or coffin: see Gen. 50:26), described as 2.5 cubits long, 1.5 cubits wide, and 1.5 cubits deep (25:10). There were two sizes of cubit in Israel, one approximately 18 inches long and the other about 24 inches in length. The box was therefore about three-and-a-half to four feet long and some two to two-and-a-half feet wide and deep. This chest was called "the ark of the covenant" or "ark of the testimony" (25:16) and was carefully crafted and lavishly decorated (25:11). It was designed to be carried on two poles; in other words, it was movable (25:12–15). (The Hebrew word rendered "ark" here [*'aron*] is not the same as that used in reference to Noah's ark [*tebah*] in Gen. 6:14.)

The ark of the covenant seems to have had various roles during the course of Israel's history. It was viewed as a symbol of God's protection and power in the midst of war (see Josh. 6:4–14; 1 Sam. 4:4–7). It also served as a kind of throne on which the invisible God was believed to sit (see 25:22) or perhaps the footstool for the heavenly king (see Ps. 99:5; 132:7; 1 Chron. 28:20). It is clear in this passage that the ark was viewed as a container built to hold the commandments that Moses had received from God (25:16, 21–22). In this capacity, the ark was a strong symbol for God's presence and Israel's obligations. When Solomon built the temple in Jerusalem centuries later, the ark of the covenant, containing the two tablets of stone on which the Ten Commandments were inscribed, was placed in the holy of holies, or the innermost part of the temple (1 Kgs. 8:3–9).

The second special item mentioned is somewhat enigmatic. In English translations it is usually called the "mercy seat" (25:17). The problem is that the Hebrew term (*kaporet*) more literally means "a cover" and is never used in reference to something to sit on, which is the usual meaning of "seat" in English. Better to envision this mercy seat as a kind of lid to place over the ark. Two cherubim facing one another were to be placed at either end of the mercy seat (25:19). These "cherubs" were not the sweet, childlike angels sometimes pictured in medieval art. Rather, they were animal-like (perhaps human but in Assyrian art they are lionlike) creatures with wings. Their wings were to spread out over the covering (25:20). The dimensions (length and width) of the covering or mercy seat were the same as those of the ark (25:17). The covering was to be carefully crafted and richly ornamented (25:17). It was then to be placed over the ark (25:21).

The function of the mercy seat is not absolutely clear. Certainly it marked the place, along with the ark, where God would meet Moses to give divine instruction (25:22). But the verbal root on which the noun translated "mercy seat" (*kapar*) is based is often used with reference to making atonement for sin (32:30; see Lev. 16:1–16). Thus, the mercy seat may well have been understood as something to deter or remedy the effects of sin.

The third piece of furniture given special attention was a small table, two cubits by one cubit by one-and-a-half cubits. It was to be made of acacia wood, which was known especially for its durability (25:23). This table was to be constructed to hold the "bread of the Presence" (NRSV). The Hebrew terms involved literally mean "the bread of faces" ("face" is frequently a euphemism for "presence"). As with the two previous items, gold was to be used generously in decorating this table (25:24–26). The table, like the ark, was designed to be mobile, to be carried on poles (25:27–28). On the table were to be utensils of various sorts that would be used to hold incense and to take care of different kinds of drink and food offerings (25:29). The table was to be set and maintained at all times (25:30).

The exact use of the table and its bread of the Presence is not certain. In ancient shrines and temples, it was common practice to bring food offerings before the resident deities. Thus, the bread of the Presence may have been a symbolic, perpetual food offering to God. On the other hand, this table might have provided the place where worshipers could actually eat together in the presence of God, binding themselves more closely to one another and to God. Of course, it may have been a combination of each of these possibilities. Whatever the case, the table with its perpetual setting of dishes and food stood as a reminder of God's ongoing care that had begun with water, quails, and manna in the wilderness.

Finally, the fourth piece of equipment singled out for special notice was a six-branched lampstand (Hebrew: *menorah*). It too was to be elaborately decorated of pure gold, with three branches coming forth from each side of the central shaft (25:31–32). The instructions for the construction of the lampstand are precise and intricate but incomplete. More detail is offered in relation to this particular piece of furniture than for any of the others (25:33–39), but the size and type of lamps to be placed on the stand, for instance, are not given. It no doubt was beautiful.

The general shape, with the branches coming out of the shaft, is reminiscent of tree images found in the ancient Near East that are symbolic of the tree of life and the tree of wisdom. Clearly it was designed to provide light in the darkened interior of the tabernacle. Light, of course, had multiple symbolic nuances, from representing the knowledge and wisdom of God to the universal presence of God. God's first act of creation was to bring light into existence (Gen. 1:3). God's ninth "wonder" was to engulf Egypt in deep darkness, "a darkness that can be felt" (Exod. 10:21). In the midst of that darkness, however, "all the Israelites had light" (10:23). The lampstand with its seven lamps supplied light continuously in the midst of actual and figurative darkness.

The Tabernacle

Detailed instructions concerning the construction of the movable shrine, the tabernacle, are provided in chapter 26. The descriptions of the various elements that were to be used, including numerous curtains and the framework on which to place them, are precise, but the terminology is obscure and very limited in usage in the Bible (26:1–29). The exact proportions are somewhat difficult to determine, but it seems that the tabernacle was to be thirty cubits long and ten cubits wide (approximately 45 feet by 15 feet). While some of the details are undecipherable, it is clear that all was designed to ensure that the tabernacle was movable.

A special curtain was to create a division within the tabernacle (26:31–32). The way the curtain was to be hung formed one section in the tabernacle that was approximately seven-and-a-half feet square. This constituted the most holy space (the "holy of holies" in later language) and formed the western end of the tabernacle. Into this most holy place, the ark of the covenant with the mercy seat was to be centered (26:33–34). On the outside of the curtain, in a space approximately seven-and-a-half wide and fifteen feet long that formed the eastern section of the tabernacle, the table of the Presence was to be placed on the north side, and the six-branched lampstand was to be situated on the south side (26:34–35).

Numerous other instructions are given, from the construction of a large, rectangular, open-air courtyard to enclose the tabernacle (27:9-19), to detailed information about the priests and their vestments (28:1–29:46) and about additional ritual equipment to be located within the tabernacle and in the surrounding courtyard (30:8). What is interesting about all of this is the degree to which it appears to be a reflection of the design of and priestly activity in the temple of Solomon, which was constructed in the middle of the tenth century—long after the time of Moses. The Babylonians destroyed that Temple in 587 BCE, and many scholars think that it provided, in retrospect, the conceptual model of the tabernacle.

The Completion of the Work

In chapters 35–39, all of the detailed instructions given in chapters 25–31 are accomplished. Each act of creation is reported, and the plan set out in the preceding chapter is completed verse by verse. This took enormous effort on the part of the people. Wood had to be collected and prepared. Sources of gold had to be found, since it is unlikely that there was enough left within the community after the golden calf debacle. There were no fabric shops or sewing machines, no power saws or tool dyes—just human ingenuity and patient labor. The human achievement here is actually quite noteworthy.

The people brought all their handiwork to Moses for his approval. When he examined their work, it was "just as the Lord had commanded Moses" (39:42). Moses was well pleased and blessed the people (39:43). How many hours and how many hands this work required are not recorded, but this was no easy job. And it met all the specifications that had been included in the plans that they had been given.

All that was needed was to erect the tabernacle, and Moses was given his marching orders. The work was to be done on "the first day of the first month"— on New Year's Day. This came about in the second year of their sojourn (40:1, 17). Moses was told to perform a series of actions each intended to sanctify the tabernacle, its furniture, and its personnel. With oil he was to anoint the tabernacle and all that was in it (40:9), as well as the altar for burnt offerings that stood in the courtyard (40:10) and the basin for cleansing that also stood in the courtyard (40:11). By this anointing, he would thereby consecrate these things for their special, holy use. He also was to wash Aaron and his sons with water, put on them the vestments prepared for them, and anoint and consecrate them as well (40:13–14).

As has become typical by this point in our study of Exodus, Moses "did everything just as the Lord had commanded him" (40:16). In a rhetorical style that may seem unnecessarily redundant from a modern standpoint, the narrator carefully and forcefully recounts Moses' actions. Each step in the erection of the tabernacle, the construction of its furniture, the installation of the priesthood, and the initiation of offerings is noted with the repetitious summary that it was done "as the LORD had commanded Moses" (40:19, 21, 23, 25, 27, 29, 32). This summary of the work of Moses has a liturgical ring to it and perhaps served that function each time the consecration of the tabernacle was recalled and celebrated.

During the construction of the tabernacle and its furnishings, Moses was conspicuously missing (chaps. 35–39). In chapter 40, however, Moses again takes center stage. By his authority, the tabernacle is declared appropriate and worthy of consecration. Moses technically establishes the priesthood of Aaron and his sons by setting them apart with anointing oil. He personally oversees the erection of the tabernacle and the appropriate placement of each of its important parts. Finally, it is Moses who "finished the work" (40:33).

The Cloud and the Glory

From the time the divine glory rested on Sinai, veiled by the heavy cloud (24:15), Moses and the people had struggled between the desire for the presence of God and the fear of it. Moses and the people constantly wanted assurance from God that God would go with them when they left Sinai. The intention of God to dwell among the people was clearly stated as part of the instructions to build a tabernacle (25:8).

However, something happened on the way to the completion of the divine plan. The people sinned grievously by fashioning a golden image of a calf and worshiping before it (32:1–6). The relationship with God that had been established was placed in jeopardy. Only by the courageous intercession of Moses did God decide to restrain the divine anger and the deserved punishment (32:11–14; 33:12–23). Then the covenant was renewed, and God reiterated the intention to go with the people to the land they were to inhabit (34:10–28).

After Moses and the people finished the assigned task of constructing a place appropriate for God's presence, they waited to see what would happen next. Would God indeed come into their midst? Did God really intend on accompanying them as the journey continued? Then, the text tells us, "the glory covered the tent of meeting [Hebrew: *'ohel mo'ed*], and the glory filled the tabernacle [Hebrew: *mishkan*]" (40:34). The cloud was not a natural phenomenon; it was that special cloud that hid, while also affirming, the divine presence on Sinai. The glory was that bright luminescence that attended the presence of God on Sinai. Because the cloud had settled (*shakan*) on the tent of meeting and because the glory had filled the tabernacle, Moses could not enter (40:35). In these two verses, the tradition of the tent of meeting (33:7–11) is brought together with the narrative about the tabernacle in such a way that they came to be considered essentially as one and the same (40:38). The tabernacle had been accepted by God as the place where the divine presence would dwell among humankind. Moses' intercession and obedience had served to ensure that God's presence would be with the people.

The tabernacle became the means by which the presence of God with Israel was assured. Nevertheless, the tabernacle was built to be portable, which signaled that God did not need nor intend to be rooted in any one particular geographic place. Whenever the cloud was "taken up," the people understood that they were to move on. So long as the cloud remained on the tabernacle, the people stayed in that place as well (40:36–37). The chapter concludes with this verse: "For the cloud of the LORD was on the tabernacle by day, and the fire was in the cloud by night, before the eyes of all the house of Israel at each stage of their journey" (40:38).

Conclusion

In the remarkable book of Exodus, the account is preserved of Israel's enslavement, deliverance, and establishment as the people of God. It comes to its conclusion with the beautiful though sometimes tedious (in the abundance of detail) description of the process of building and erecting the tabernacle, the tent of meeting, where the divine presence came to "tent" (*shakan*) among them. The hope for God's protecting and sustaining presence was realized. At the same time, the shrine was built to be movable, in keeping with God's intention to be always on the go. God would be with them, but they would have to go where God wanted to go. The people of Israel ministered before the presence of God, but they never controlled it. The freedom of God was preserved, while the longing for the assurance of divine care was met.

Part Two

LEADER'S GUIDE

DONALD L. GRIGGS

Guidelines for
Bible Study Leaders

The Bible from Scratch Series

This is one of a series of Bible study courses designed for people who want to study the Bible but who are reluctant to join a group of Bible study veterans. Many fear they will be embarrassed and will not be able to use the Bible and participate comfortably. This series, however, makes no assumptions regarding what someone should know regarding the Bible, and that is why this is identified as a course for beginners. Many who come to your class, however, will not be beginners with the Bible but will have a desire to engage in a course that deals with the basics for Bible study.

Goals of the Course

Even though this course on Exodus could be read and studied without one's being a member of a class, the greatest value of the study will be realized when the reader is engaged with others who are companions on the journey. As I prepared these session plans, I had in mind the following five goals that I hope participants will experience as a result of their study:

- Participants will bring to their study a desire to enter more deeply into the world of the Bible—specifically in this study, the world of Exodus.

- Class members will enjoy studying the Bible with others.

- Participants will come to a greater understanding and appreciation of the origins, structure, and message of Exodus.

- Prompted by what they read and think, class members will share their insights, questions, and affirmations with one another.

- Participants will develop a discipline of reading and studying the Bible on a regular basis.

Basic Teaching Principles

As I prepared these session plans, I tried to implement a number of basic principles for effective teaching and leading. The foundational principle is an attempt to involve everyone in the class in as many activities as possible during every session. It is not possible to succeed with everyone every session, but there are many opportunities for individuals to participate, and most will if they are encouraged to do so. You will see this principle present in all the session plans that follow. I had another ten principles in mind as I designed this course:

- The leader does not have to be an expert but serves best as companion and guide.

- The leader provides sufficient information but not so much that participants lose the joy of discovery.

- Motivation for learning involves enjoying the process, completing tasks, and making choices.

- Participants learn best when a variety of activities and resources are used to appeal to their different interests, needs, and learning styles.

- Participants need to be invited to express their feelings, ideas, and beliefs in creative ways that are appropriate to them and to the subject matter.

- All participants need opportunities to share what they understand and believe.

- Open-ended questions invite interpretation, reflection, and application.

- Persons are nurtured in faith when they share their faith stories with one another.

- All teaching and learning happens in planned and unplanned ways and is for the purpose of increasing biblical literacy and faithful discipleship.

- The Bible becomes the living word of God when teachers and learners see their own faith stories expressed in Scripture.

Room Arrangement

Arrange the room where you meet in such a way that participants are seated at tables; this will allow them to have space for their Bibles, other materials, and coffee cups. Tables also send the message that we are going to work, that we will not just sit and listen to a lecture. If members of the group do not know other members by name, they all need name tags. Set up a table with hot water and the makings for coffee, tea, and hot chocolate just inside the entrance to the room so that everyone can get a cup and then find a seat. If you have a small group, arrange the tables in a rectangle or square so that everyone can see all the other members of the group. With a small group, you will be able to be seated with them. If you have a large group, arrange the tables in a fan shape pointed toward the front so the participants can see the leader standing at the front of the group with a lectern or small table and a whiteboard, newsprint easel, or bulletin board.

Resources

On the first week, be sure to provide Bibles for those who do not bring one. Continue to provide Bibles for those activities when it is important for everyone to have the same translation and edition if you plan for them all to look at the same pages at the same time. However, continue to encourage participants to bring their own Bibles. In addition to the Bibles, borrow from the church library, the pastor's library, and your own library copies of Bible dictionaries, Exodus commentaries, and Bible atlases. A church library will not ordinarily have enough Bible reference works for each person. For those sessions where members are responsible for researching a passage, person, or event in Exodus, make photocopies of the appropriate materials from a Bible dictionary, encyclopedia, or atlas. For one-time use, for one class, this is not a violation of copyright laws.

Be sure to provide paper and pencils for those who don't bring them. Almost all the activity sheets to be used by the participants are at the end of the respective session plans for which they will be used. This means that each participant needs to have a copy of this course book. If some class members cannot afford to purchase a copy or prefer not to, arrange to have several copies available for them to borrow.

Time

I planned each session to be an hour in length. If you have less than an hour, you will have to make adjustments. It will be better to leave out an activity than to rush class members through all the suggested activities. Perhaps it would be possible in your situation to schedule more than seven sessions. There is probably enough material here for eight to ten sessions. If you can arrange for additional sessions, you would truly be able to deal with everything carefully, without hurrying.

If you and your group have not already studied the first two books in this Bible study series, *The Bible from Scratch: The Old Testament for Beginners* or *The Bible from Scratch: The New Testament for Beginners*, you may find it helpful to use session 1 from either of those courses as an introduction to this style of Bible study.

Final Word

As you prepare to teach this course, read each chapter of the Participant's Guide as you consider your teaching strategy for each session. You should assume that many, though not all, of the participants will have read the respective passages before coming to the session, and you should be as familiar with the material as they are. Exploring Exodus with fellow pilgrims on the journey of faith will be for them and for you a challenging, inspiring, and satisfying experience. May God bless you with many discoveries and much joy on this journey. If you and the members of your Bible study group have found this course to be helpful, you may want to look for other Bible studies in the series.

Session One

In Pharaoh's Egypt

A Study of Exodus 1:1—2:25

BEFORE THE SESSION

Focus of the Session

In this first session, it will be important to get started on the right foot by welcoming everyone, helping them get acquainted with one another, and introducing the course of study. There is one major exploring activity that will enable the participants to connect with the characters and context of the first two chapters of Exodus.

Advance Preparation

- Read the selected portions of Exodus for this session.

- If you read through the whole book of Exodus, you will find that that will provide the background and perspective for understanding the selected portions.

- Read an introductory article or two about the book of Exodus in a study Bible, Bible dictionary, or Bible commentary.

- Read articles in a Bible dictionary on the documentary hypothesis, the Hebrews, Moses, and Egypt.

- Display a map of Egypt at the time of Moses in order to show the locations of Pithom and Ramses. There may be a set of Bible maps in the church school or a Bible atlas in the church library that you could borrow. Many Bibles also have maps in the back.

- Provide a few extra Bibles for those who forget to bring one.

- Research sources and prices of study Bibles, preferably ones that use the NRSV, which is the translation on which this study is based. Share this information with the group after you explain the value of using a study Bible. (See the list of recommended study Bibles in the appendix on pp. 124–25.)

- Write the words of the Doxology on a sheet of newsprint or whiteboard.

Physical Arrangements

Reread "Guidelines for Bible Study Leaders," which offers suggestions on room arrangement, resources and materials, and refreshments. Have everything ready for the first session. You will want to get off to a good start, especially for those who are new to Bible study.

Teaching Alternatives

The session plan that follows assumes a minimum of an hour for the study. If you have less than an hour, then you will need to make some adjustments in the plan: (1) extend the session to two sessions, (2) skip the community-building activity if the members of the group already know each other fairly well, or (3) eliminate the longer of the two closing activities.

DURING THE SESSION
Welcoming the Participants

Arrive early enough to set up the refreshments and to have everything ready before the first persons arrive. Ask participants to sign in and make name tags for themselves. Greet each one by name and with a warm welcome. As group members gather, remind them of the five goals on page 64. Check to see who needs to borrow a Bible, and give them one. Also, encourage them to bring a Bible next week. If any of the participants do not already have a copy of this course book, give them one so that they will have access to it during the session, especially to the activity sheets.

Introducing the Course

After all have arrived and you have welcomed them, share with them an overview of this course. Here are some points to emphasize:

- This first session will focus on the situation of the Israelites in Egypt, introduce the main character of the book, Moses, and explore the context of Moses in Midian.

- The remaining six sessions will focus on selected narratives in Exodus in chronological order. The narratives of the forty chapters of Exodus are too many to deal with in a short course. However, the narratives that are chosen will provide a helpful overview of the whole book.

- The session plans will not necessarily repeat what is in the Participant's Guide but will be based on that material and the related passages of Exodus.

- It is expected that the participants will read the relevant chapter in the Participant's Guide in preparation for each session.

- Everyone should bring a Bible to class, preferably a study Bible.

- Reading the selected passages in preparation for each session will enhance greatly the understanding and appreciation of Exodus.

- Each session will include a presentation by the leader, but most of the time the leader will guide participants through a series of activities designed to engage them with the key Scriptures and main ideas of the session.

- There are no dumb questions. All questions are appropriate. Encourage the participants to ask questions of the leader and the group.

- Everyone's insights, ideas, and affirmations will be received and respected. It is important to feel free to express what is in one's mind and heart.

Opening Prayer

Introduce this activity by stating that in each session there will be an opening prayer prompted by words from Scripture, often from the book of Psalms. This session's opening prayer from Psalm 25 is to be prayed in unison.

- Introduce Psalm 25 as a prayer of David seeking God's guidance and forgiveness.

- Direct participants to page 74, where they will find Psalm 25:1–10, or to their Bibles if there are enough copies of the NRSV.

- Pray in unison Psalm 25:1–10.

- After the prayer, ask participants to select a phrase, line, or verse that speaks to them in a special way.

- Invite those who are willing to share without comment the words they have chosen.

Building Community among the Participants

In this first session, take a little time for persons to get acquainted with other members of the group. Invite group members to introduce themselves by stating three things: their name, a memory of a Sunday school or adult class they attended in the past, and a favorite story in the Bible (in Exodus, if they remember any of the narratives in that book). Introduce yourself as well, perhaps even first in order to model what you have in mind. After all have been introduced, affirm what has been shared and indicate that you have heard some wonderful memories and favorite Bible stories and that this is a great foundation on which to build this study of the book of Exodus.

Introducing Exodus

Spend a few minutes making a brief introduction to the book of Exodus. Consider including the following in your presentation:

- Explain the origin of the title of the book.

- Mention that there are two major sections of the book: Exodus 1:1–15:21, which deals with the Israelites in Egypt, the plagues, and the Israelites' escape; and Exodus 15:22–40:38, which presents all the narratives of the wilderness journey. The first section features God's power at work in the midst of the events as they unfold, and the second section shows the divine presence accompanying the people during their journey.

- Help participants make the transition from the setting of Genesis 50 to that of Exodus 1.

- Show on a map the location of the cities of Pithom and Ramses.

- Review how Exodus is a composite of several traditions gathered in this one book over a period of several centuries. Make reference to the Participant's Guide, pages 5–6.

- If you feel that you have sufficient time, that you think the group will not be sidetracked, and that you are comfortable with the subject, spend a few minutes discussing the documentary hypothesis.

Reviewing the Opening Narratives

The narratives in the first two chapters of Exodus span a period of several decades. The situation of the Israelites in Egypt is presented, the birth and saving of a Hebrew boy is described, and an adult Moses is introduced. The Participant's Guide provides an excellent summary of this material. In this activity, the goal is to engage the members of the group in a process of personal identification with various characters in the narrative. Toward that end, do the following:

- Direct participants to page 75 and the activity sheet "Identifying with Characters in the Narrative." The instructions are self-explanatory, but review and reinforce them.

- Either assign each person one of the nine characters, or invite participants to make their own choice of which character will be their focus. If there are fewer than nine members in the group, eliminate one or more characters. It will be good for the leader to select a character. If there are more than nine members, double up on one or more characters.

- Remind group members that there are no correct or incorrect words; rather, they are to use their imaginations as they speak from the roles of their characters.

- Allow five to eight minutes for group members to read and reflect on their passages.

- Invite participants to introduce their characters, in the order presented on the activity sheet, by speaking in the first person. They are to describe the setting in which they find themselves, speak about what they are thinking or feeling as their character, and give some idea as to why they acted in the way they did.

- After all participants have introduced themselves, thank them for taking such a risk in this first session.

- Guide the group in a time of reflection with questions such as these:

  What impressions or feelings do you have as a result of speaking from the first-person perspective of a character in the narrative?

  What are some insights that have come to you about the context of the Israelites in Egypt?

  How do you see God at work in these two chapters?

  What do you think the writer is trying to communicate regarding God's power being expressed in the affairs of individuals as well as groups of people?

  What questions come to mind as a result of this exercise?

Closing

There are two possibilities for closing the session. If you are running short on time, sing together the "Doxology." If you have five to ten minutes remaining, return to Psalm 25:1–10, which was used as the opening prayer. Instruct participants to return to the phrases, lines, or verses they had said were important to them, and ask them to write those words on a sheet of paper. Ask them to continue writing a sentence or two as their prayer. Invite those who are willing to share their prayers. After each has spoken, invite the whole group to respond, "O God, hear our prayer."

AFTER THE SESSION

Encourage the participants to read chapter 2 of the Participant's Guide, "Who Did You Say You Were?" and Exodus 3:1–6:30.

A Prayer of David and Our Prayer

(Psalm 25:1-10)

To you, O LORD, I lift up my soul.
O, my God, in you I trust;
    do not let me be put to shame;
    do not let my enemies exult over me.
Do not let those who wait for you be put to shame;
    let them be ashamed who are wantonly treacherous.

Make me know your ways, O LORD;
    teach me your paths.
Lead me in your truth, and teach me;
    for you are the God of my salvation;
    for you I wait all day long.

Be mindful of you mercy, O LORD, and of your steadfast love,
    for they have been from of old.
Do not remember the sins of my youth or my transgressions;
    according to your steadfast love remember me,
    for your goodness' sake, O LORD!

Good and upright is the LORD;
    therefore he instructs sinners in the way.
He leads the humble in what is right,
    and teaches the humble his way.
All the paths of the LORD are steadfast love and faithfulness,
    for those who keep his covenant and his decrees.

Identifying with Characters in the Narrative

Instructions: Focus on one of the following nine characters. Read the short passage related to your character. Then answer the questions below.

Nine Characters in the Narrative:

Egyptian Pharaoh	Exodus 1:1–22
Oppressed Israelite	Exodus 1:8–22
Midwife Shiphrah	Exodus 1:15–22
Moses' Mother	Exodus 2:1–10
Moses' Sister	Exodus 2:1–10
Pharaoh's Daughter	Exodus 2:5–10
Moses	Exodus 2:11–22
The Priest of Midian	Exodus 2:15b–22
Zipporah	Exodus 2:15b–22

Questions:

1. What might the character be thinking or feeling about his or her situation?

_____

_____

2. Why might the character have acted the way he/she did? Be prepared to speak in the role of your character. It is OK to use a little "holy" imagination.

_____

_____

Session Two

Who Did You Say You Were?

A Study of Exodus 3:1–6:30

BEFORE THE SESSION
Focus of the Session

In this session, the primary focus will be on God's calling Moses in the Midian desert and Moses' reluctance to respond to God's call. Through several activities, participants will be able to make connections between the biblical texts and their own faith and life journeys.

Advance Preparation

- Read the selected portions of Exodus for this session.

- Read the comments and notes of the selected passage in a study Bible or commentary.

- Obtain a Bible lands map so that you can show the approximate location of Midian, the land to which Moses fled.

- Research in a Bible dictionary, wordbook, or commentary the holy name for God that was revealed to Moses at the burning bush.

- Provide hymnals for singing a hymn during the closing, or print out the words to the hymn "Here I Am, Lord."

- Prepare the activity sheet suggested for the closing prayer.

- Provide a few extra Bibles for those who forget to bring one.

Teaching Alternatives

The session plan that follows assumes a minimum of an hour for the study. If you have less than an hour, then you will need to make some adjustments in the plan: (1) extend the session to two sessions, (2) eliminate the segment "Considering Moses' Excuses," and/or (3) eliminate the longer of the two closing activities.

DURING THE SESSION
Welcoming the Participants

Arrive at class early enough to be sure that refreshments, room arrangement, and all materials are ready before the first persons arrive. Greet everyone as they arrive, and be alert to any new persons who were not at the first session. Ask participants to sign in and make name tags for themselves, which is especially important if there are any new group members. Give new members a copy of the course book and a Bible if they did not bring one, and assure them that they will catch on quickly with the content and process of the class.

Opening Prayer

A major focus of this session is God's call of Moses while he is tending his father-in-law's sheep in the Midian desert. God gets Moses' attention through a burning bush that is not consumed by the flame. God calls Moses to return to Egypt to be the instrument by which the Israelites will be led from their oppression into the land of God's promise. There are a number of call narratives in the Old Testament, some of which are included in this opening prayer. After participants have arrived, made their name tags, and found their seats, call the group together for an opening prayer:

- Introduce the prayer by stating that in addition to God's call of Moses that is featured in this session, there are other call narratives in the Old Testament. The litany prayer will include brief excerpts from passages of several of those calls.

- Direct participants to the litany on page 83 in the Leader's Guide.

- Invite participants to take turns reading the biblical passages, with everyone responding in unison with the prayer response.

After sharing the litany, spend a few minutes reflecting on one or two of the following questions:

- Even though these are short excerpts from larger narratives, what do you see as similarities in these quotes from the several call narratives?

- What do you see as significant differences?

- How relevant is the experience of God's calling these Old Testament characters to God's calling persons today for opportunities of service?

Reviewing Session One

Spend a few minutes reviewing the previous session for the sake of those who were not present and to take advantage of the reading everyone else did. Be sure not to get sidetracked in this activity, because there is a lot to cover in this session.

- Start by asking, "What are some key points of the transition between the end of Genesis and the beginning of Exodus?"

- Ask a second question: "What was the situation of the Israelites in Egypt, and who are some of the key characters in the first two chapters of Exodus?"

Setting the Stage of God's Call of Moses

Use a Bible map to show the possible location of the Midian desert where God appeared to Moses while he was tending his father-in-law's sheep. Also, show the locations of the peoples that are mentioned in Exodus 3:8. Share any information you have gathered regarding the typical terrain and plants of the Midian desert.

Identifying with Moses Being Called by God

To set the stage for a little role identification, engage the participants in a brief time of brainstorming two different perspectives on Moses' response to God's call to return to Egypt. Guide the group in the following steps:

- On two sheets of newsprint or two columns on a white-board, write two headings: "Reasons for Moses to Stay in Midian" and "Reasons for Moses to Return to Egypt."

- Spend a few minutes brainstorming reasons for each list. You should have four to eight reasons on each list before proceeding to the next step.

- Ask participants to work in pairs. One member of the pair is to identify with Moses' reluctance to return to Egypt, and the other member is to identify with Moses' willingness to return to Egypt.

- Tell participants that they are to put themselves in Moses' sandals, to take on the role of Moses from the perspective each has chosen.

- You, the leader, will read Exodus 3:1–11a, stopping after the words "But Moses said to God . . ."

- The pairs of participants are then to imagine that together they are Moses debating within himself how to respond to God. They are to spend just a couple of minutes expressing their thoughts and feelings about whether or not to return to Egypt. This is like when we debate in our own minds when faced with making a difficult decision.

After a few minutes, engage the whole group in a discussion guided by questions such as these or ones you have created:

- What are some feelings and thoughts you have as a result of identifying with Moses in being called by God to return to Egypt?

- How realistic is the dilemma Moses faced?

- When have you felt called by God for a task, and how have you struggled with that call?

- What thoughts and feelings did you have when making the decision to respond to God's call?

Reflecting on God's Holy Name

Informed by your research, make a brief presentation about God's holy name. Consider including in your presentation the following:

- Emphasize the importance of names in the Old Testament context.

- Explain the reason why it was important to Moses to know the name of the God who was calling him to return to Egypt.

- Refer to pages 15–16 in the Participant's Guide for information on this topic.

- Review the meaning of "I AM WHO I AM" and the several forms it can take.

- Explain the significance of "YHWH" and how this holy name is rendered as "the LORD" when translated in English Bibles.

- Explain that because of the commandment not to misuse the name of God, Jews today do not speak the holy name of God but rather substitute a Hebrew word, *Adonai,* translated as "Lord" in English.

Considering Moses' Excuses

Summarize this material with a brief presentation. Exodus 3–4 shows that Moses was reluctant to accept God's call. He offers four excuses for why he cannot do what God is asking:

1. "Who am I that I should go to Pharaoh?" (3:11).

2. "If they ask what is his [God's] name, what shall I say to them?" (3:13).

3. "But suppose they do not believe me or listen to me" (4:1).

4. "I have never been eloquent. . . . O, my Lord, please send someone else" (4:10, 13).

Call attention to how God responds to each of Moses' excuses:

1. "I will be with you" (3:12).

2. "I AM WHO I AM" (3:14).

3. God provides a staff with indwelling power (4:2–9).

4. "The anger of the LORD was kindled against Moses, and he said, 'What of your brother Aaron?'" (4:14).

Spend a few minutes guiding the group in discussing one or more questions such as those that follow, or create your own questions to guide the discussion.

• What fears or concerns of Moses do these four excuses represent?

• How relevant are these excuses to our own faith journeys?

• When have you had a sense that God was calling you? What kinds of excuses did you have?

Reviewing Moses' and Aaron's Encounters with Pharaoh

In chapters 5 and 6, we see the beginning of the struggles between Moses/Aaron and Pharaoh, between Moses/Aaron and the Israelites, and between Moses and God. Guide the group through the following steps:

• Divide the group into three smaller groups.

• Assign each group to search chapters 5 and 6 for evidence of one of these struggles:

Group 1—The struggle between Moses/Aaron and Pharaoh

Group 2—The struggle between Moses/Aaron and the Israelites

Group 3—The struggle between Moses and God

- Ask each group to identify its parties' positions, and write the responses on a sheet of newsprint or a whiteboard.

- Conclude the activity with a discussion that responds to this question: "What do you see as the writer's over-arching theme or purpose in the narrative?"

Closing

There are two possibilities for closing the session. If you have enough time, you can lead the group through both activities.

1. If at least one person is comfortable leading the group in singing, sing one or more stanzas from the familiar hymn "Here I Am, Lord." Have either hymnals or a printout of the words on hand.

2. Prepare an activity sheet with the following written on it: "_____, I am the God of your ancestors and your God. I have seen the needs in your family, community, and church. I will send you as my representative to respond to _____." Distribute the activity sheets, and encourage participants to fill in the first blank with their name and to fill in the second blank with a need that is on their heart. Conclude with a time of silence as participants read what they have written. End the silence with an invitation: "And all God's people say . . ." The participants will respond with a loud "Amen."

AFTER THE SESSION

Encourage participants to read chapter 3 of the Participant's Guide, "Let My People Go" and the corresponding passages: Exodus 7:1–25; 11:1–12:42; and 14:1–15:21.

God Calls Servants: A Litany

Now the LORD said to Abram, "Go from your country and your kindred and your father's house to the land that I will show you. I will make of you a great nation, and I will bless you, and make your name great, so that you will be a blessing." . . . So Abram went, as the LORD had told him. . . . He was seventy-five years old when he left Haran (Gen. 12:1-2, 4).

> *Gracious God, help us to be open to hear your call to us to leave a familiar place in order to follow you as you lead us into new opportunities of service.*

Jacob dreamed that there was a ladder set up on earth, the top of it reaching to heaven; and the angels of God were ascending and descending on it. And the LORD stood beside him and said, "I am the LORD, the God of Abraham your father. . . . Know that I am with you and will keep you wherever you go." . . . Jacob said, "Surely the LORD is in this place—and I did not know it!" (Gen. 28:12–16).

> *Ever-present God, we thank you for your continued presence in our lives and for assuring us that you will be with us no matter where we are or where we go.*

God called Moses out of the bush, "Moses, Moses!" And he said, "Here I am." . . . The LORD said to Moses, "I have observed the misery of my people who are in Egypt. . . . So come, I will send you to Pharaoh to bring my people, the Israelites, out of Egypt." But Moses said to God, "Who am I that I should go to Pharaoh, and bring the Israelites out of Egypt?" God said, "I will be with you" (Exod. 3:4, 7, 10–12).

> *Calling God, we sense your call to us to do important work for you, yet we feel that we are unprepared and unable to do what you ask of us. Be patient with us as we sort through our priorities and commitments in responding to your call.*

God spoke to Joshua, "My servant Moses is dead. Now proceed across the Jordan, you and all this people, into the land that I am giving to them, to the Israelites. . . . As I was with Moses, so I will be with you; I will not fail you or forsake you. . . . Be strong and courageous; do not be frightened or dismayed, for the LORD your God is with you wherever you go" (Josh. 1:2, 6, 9).

> *Faithful God, help us to be strong and courageous when you call us to launch out into the unknown. We trust that you will be with us every step of the way.*

The angel of the LORD appeared to Gideon and said to him, "The LORD is with you, you mighty warrior." Gideon answered, "But sir, if the LORD is with us, why then has all this happened to us?" . . . The LORD said, "Go in this might of yours and deliver Israel from the hand of Midian; I hereby commission you." Gideon said, "How can I deliver Israel? My clan is the weakest in Manasseh, and I am the least in my family." The LORD said, "But I will be with you" (Judg. 6:12–16).

> *God of infinite patience, you call us to serve you with the wisdom and gifts we possess, yet we often doubt that we are the ones to do what you ask of us. Help us, O God, to trust you. Amen.*

Session Three

Let My People Go

A Study of Exodus 7:1–25; 11:1–12:42; 14:1–15:21

BEFORE THE SESSION
Focus of the Session

There is a lot of material to cover in this session. The signs and wonders performed by God and the subsequent escape from Egypt will be the two main emphases of this session.

Advance Preparation

- Read the selected portions of Exodus for this session.

- Read the comments and notes on the passages in a study Bible or commentary.

- Have on hand a Bible lands map to show the approximate location of Ramses, Succoth, and the Sea of Reeds (Red Sea).

- Research Passover, sacrifice, the Sea of Reeds or the Red Sea, and the pillars of cloud and fire in a Bible dictionary, wordbook, or commentary.

- Gather as many Bible translations as you can find in order to compare Exodus 7:3 and 7:13 as suggested in the third activity after the opening prayer. You can also access a variety of translations at www.biblegateway.com.

- Provide hymnals for singing a hymn during the closing, or print out the words to the hymn "Go Down Moses."

- Provide a few extra Bibles for those who forget to bring one.

- Consider inviting a rabbi from a nearby synagogue to be your guest for an additional session in which he or she can provide a more in-depth understanding of the Passover narrative in Exodus as well as explain how Jewish communities understand and celebrate Passover today.

Teaching Alternatives

The session plan that follows assumes a minimum of an hour for the study, and there are probably too many activities for one session. If you have less than an hour or if you would like to do all the activities and not be rushed, you will need to either extend the session to two sessions or eliminate one or more of the activities.

DURING THE SESSION
Welcoming the Participants

Welcome any newcomers, give them a copy of the course book, and assure them that they will catch on quickly with the content and the process of the class session. Check to see who needs a Bible and give them one, and encourage them to bring a Bible next week.

Opening Prayer

Five psalms (78, 105, 106, 135, and 136) are identified as "Salvation History Psalms" or "Psalms of the Mighty Acts of God." Each one includes passages that focus on the subject of this week's study, the Lord's victory over Pharaoh and his army. The first twelve verses of Psalm 106 serve as the prompting of this session's opening prayer. Invite the group to join in the opening prayer as follows:

- Direct the participants to page 90 in the Leader's Guide, "The Psalmist's Prayer and Our Prayer." There are two options for reading these verses. One is to divide into two groups, with one group reading the odd-numbered verses and the other group reading the even-numbered verses. The second is for the participants to read the passage silently.

- After reading the verses from Psalm 106, ask the members of the group to each select a phrase, line, or verse that speaks to them at that moment.

- Invite those who are willing to share what they chose. After each has spoken, ask the group to say in unison, "God's steadfast love endures forever."

- Discuss this question: "What do these verses tell us about God and God's people?"

Reviewing Session Two

Spend a few minutes reviewing the previous session for the sake of those who were not present and to take advantage of the reading everyone else did:

- Start by asking, "What are some things you remember about Moses' response to God's call?"

- Discuss a second question: "How significant is it for you that God's own name was revealed to Moses?"

Getting Oriented Geographically

Using a Bible map, spend a few minutes identifying the geographical locations that are mentioned in the chapters of Exodus for this session. The important sites to identify are Ramses, Succoth, the Sea of Reeds, and the Red Sea. Keep the map available for reference during the session.

Comparing Several Translations

In the Participant's Guide, pages 22–23, W. Eugene March deals with a Hebrew word that is translated in the NRSV as "harden" in reference to Pharaoh's heart. In this activity, take a few minutes to look at Exodus 7:3 and 7:13, which are representative of all the other instances where the word appears. In addition to the several translations the participants have, obtain other translations or download the selected verses from translations found on the Internet.

The main focus of this brief activity is to illustrate March's point regarding the translation of the Hebrew word rendered as "harden" in English. As March explains, several translators suggest the idea of stubbornness on Pharaoh's part (Contemporary English Version, Common English Version, *The Message*, Today's English Version, and the Jewish Publication Society's *Tanakh*). After looking at the comparisons, discuss briefly this question: "When you read that 'Pharaoh was stubborn' instead of 'Pharaoh's heart was hardened,' what difference does it make for your understanding of the text?"

Exploring God's Signs and Wonders

The suggested reading for this session did not include chapters 8–10, which present the second through the ninth plagues. In this activity, participants will work in small groups to explore the first nine plagues. Guide the group using the following process:

- Summarize the points made by March in the Participant's Guide, pages 24–25, where he makes a distinction between plagues on the one hand, and signs and wonders on the other.

- Direct participants to page 91 of the Leader's Guide and to the activity sheet "Exploring Nine Signs and Wonders of God."

- Divide the nine passages among the group members. If you have fewer than nine in your group, omit one or more of the signs and wonders.

- The small groups will spend about ten minutes reading their assigned passages and reflecting on the four questions.

- Call the small groups back together, and ask them to each report their answers. Receive the reports from all groups one question at a time.

After all the reports have been given, guide the group in a discussion of one or more questions, such as these:

- What do you see as similarities and differences in these narratives in terms of the words and actions of Moses/Aaron and Pharaoh?

- The narratives show a prolonged struggle between the power and authority of Pharaoh and the power and authority of God. How would you characterize this struggle?

- What relevance, if any, do you see regarding the message of these passages to our faith and life today?

Reflecting on the Escape from Egypt

Exodus 11:1–14:31 contains the account of the Israelites' escape from Egypt. The best way to cover this extensive narrative will be to do a combination of guided reading and brief presentations. Your reading of notes in a study Bible or commentary will prepare you to provide explanations of the several topics. Consider the following possibilities:

- Review the instructions for the first Passover.

- Call attention to the two narratives regarding the Passover from two different sources: 12:1–28 and 12:43–13:10.

- Comment on the symbolic meaning of the sacrificial lamb, the blood, the unleavened bread, and the bitter herbs.

- Ask if any members have had the opportunity to celebrate the Passover with Jewish friends or family members. If so, ask them to share their memories and impressions of those experiences.

- Make reference to the pillars of cloud by day and of fire by night (13:21) as a sign of God's presence and protection. Ask participants to identify other passages in the Bible that they recall where either cloud or fire symbolizes God's presence and protection.

- Ask participants how they have envisioned the Israelites' crossing of the Red Sea.

- Show on a Bible lands map where the Red Sea is in relation to the supposed route of the exodus.

- Notice in the NRSV that every time "Red Sea" appears there is a footnote that mentions "Sea of Reeds." Ask what image a Sea of Reeds would evoke.

- Look at Exodus 14:10–14, which records the first of many complaints the Israelites express to Moses. Tell the group that there will be other complaints during the Israelites' forty-years' journey.

- Read in unison Exodus 14:30–31.

Conclude this activity with discussion of two questions:

- How would you summarize the Exodus authors' essential message in this section of the book?

- What do you think is the relevance of these narratives to the faith and life of oppressed believers today?

Closing

There are two possibilities for closing the session:

- If one or more persons in the group are comfortable leading the group in singing, sing several stanzas from the familiar hymn "Go Down Moses." Have hymnals or a printout of the words on hand.

- Select four to six lines from "the song of Moses" in Exodus 15:1–18 that you consider appropriate to share with the group as a closing prayer. Read one line at a time, inviting the group to repeat that line in unison.

AFTER THE SESSION

Encourage participants to read chapter 4 of the Participant's Guide, "Are We There Yet?" and Exodus 15:22–18:27.

The Psalmist's Prayer and Our Prayer

(Psalm 106:1–12)

[1]Praise the LORD!
　O give thanks to the LORD, for he is good;
　for his steadfast love endures forever.
[2]Who can utter the mighty doings of the LORD,
　or declare all his praise?
[3]Happy are those who observe justice,
　who do righteousness at all times.

[4]Remember me, O LORD, when you show favor to your people;
　help me when you deliver them;
[5]that I may see the prosperity of your chosen ones,
　that I may rejoice in the gladness of your nation,
　that I may glory in your heritage.

[6]Both we and our ancestors have sinned;
　we have committed iniquity, have done wickedly.
[7]Our ancestors, when they were in Egypt,
　did not consider your wonderful works;
they did not remember the abundance of your steadfast love,
　but rebelled against the Most High at the Red Sea.
[8]Yet he saved them for his name's sake,
　so that he might make known his mighty power.
[9]He rebuked the Red Sea, and it became dry;
　he led them through the deep as through a desert.
[10]So he saved them from the hand of the foe,
　and delivered them from the hand of the enemy.
[11]The waters covered their adversaries;
　not one of them was left.
[12]Then they believed his words;
　they sang his praise. Amen.

Exploring Nine Signs and Wonders of God

Instructions: Work individually or in small groups. Each group will work with one of the nine passages. Read the assigned passage in order to answer the four questions below.

Nine Signs and Wonders of God:

Water Turned to Blood	Exodus 7:14–25
Frogs	Exodus 8:1–15
Gnats	Exodus 8:16–19
Flies	Exodus 8:20–32
Livestock Diseased	Exodus 9:1–7
Boils	Exodus 9:8–12
Thunder and Hail	Exodus 9:13–35
Locusts	Exodus 10:1–20
Darkness	Exodus 10:21–29

Questions:

1. What do Moses and Aaron say to Pharaoh?

    _____

    _____

2. What were the responses of Pharaoh and of others, if any?

    _____

    _____

3. What were Moses' and/or Aaron's responses, if any?

    _____

    _____

4. How long did the sign last?

    _____

    _____

Session Four

Are We There Yet?

A Study of Exodus 15:22–18:27

BEFORE THE SESSION
Focus of the Session

There are three important events in the Exodus narrative of this session: (1) manna from heaven, with quails for meat, (2) water from a rock, and (3) wise words from Moses' father-in-law, Jethro. The major activity of the session will be to explore the significance of bread and water by making connections with Jesus' words when he said, "I am the bread of life," and "Those who drink the water I give them will never be thirsty." We will also spend time reviewing the role of Jethro, Moses' father-in-law.

Advance Preparation

- Read the selected portions of Exodus for this session.
- Read the comments and notes of the selected passage in a study Bible or commentary.

- Research manna, water, Jethro, and the mountain of God in a Bible dictionary, wordbook, or commentary.

- Rehearse in your mind the sequence of steps in the opening prayer activity so that you can lead it easily.

- Write on a sheet of newsprint the response for the opening prayer.

- Prepare an outline of key events from the previous session in order to prompt the participants in the activity to review session 3.

- Provide a few extra Bibles for those who forget to bring one.

DURING THE SESSION
Opening Prayer

The Exodus passages for this session show that the Israelites had a difficult time trusting God as well as trusting God's servants, Moses and Aaron. For the opening prayer, the class members will consider the theme of trusting God that permeates the book of Psalms.

- Introduce the opening prayer by speaking about the element of trust that was lacking among the Israelites and their need to trust God and God's servants, Moses and Aaron.

- Ask participants to turn to the book of Psalms. Wherever they find themselves in Psalms will be the right place.

- Direct them to spend five minutes skimming psalms, either forward or backward from where they are, searching for verses that express trust, confidence, or faith in God.

- Explain that when they find a verse or two that speaks to them, they are to mark it with their finger or a slip of paper and continuing skimming.

- After five minutes, invite participants to share the verses they have selected. After each participant shares, lead the whole group in this response: "Gracious God, increase our trust in you." (It will be helpful to have this response visible on a sheet of newsprint.)

- When the litany prayer is completed, lead the group in a discussion of one question: "When were some times when trusting God was important to you?"

Reviewing Session Three

Spend a few minutes reviewing the previous session for the sake of those who were not present and to take advantage of the reading everyone else did:

- Start by stating, "We are going to do a quick retelling of the major events we studied in the last session."

- Begin the narrative by saying, "Aaron threw down his staff and it became a snake. Pharaoh's magicians did the same, but Aaron's snake swallowed up their snakes."

- Invite participants to continue the narrative with brief statements in their own words. Continue the narrative, trying to cover all the key events and themes. Participants will likely need some prompting, so have in hand an outline of the events that were part of the previous session.

- Discuss one question: "How would you summarize the main theme or themes of this portion of the Exodus narrative?"

Exploring the Importance of Provisions for Life and Faith

This activity focuses on God's provision of manna and water in Exodus 16–17. We will also relate this to Jesus' words about bread and water. Follow this process:

- Review with the group the events in the desert when the Israelites complained about the lack of bread to eat and water to drink, which resulted in a miraculous response by God to provide for their needs. Talk your way through the narrative rather than reading the two chapters.

- Ask participants what they remember from the Gospels of Jesus making reference to bread and water. This will serves as a transition to the work they will do in two or more small groups.

- Divide the group into two smaller groups. If you have more than twelve in your group, divide it into three or more smaller groups.

- Direct participants to the activity sheet "Exploring Manna/Bread and Water" on page 98 in the Leader's Guide.

- After fifteen to twenty minutes for the groups to do their work, ask them to return to the whole group to share the results of their discussion of the two questions.

- To conclude, ask one additional question: "Bread and water are absolutely necessary for survival. In what ways do bread and water as metaphors provide insight into our spiritual lives?"

Reflecting on the Role of Jethro

The third major narrative for this session is chapter 18, which includes the appearance of Jethro and the wise advice he offers to Moses. Review this chapter with the group. Be sure to include the following:

- Moses met Jethro when he escaped from Egypt after killing a man who had mistreated a fellow Hebrew. Moses married Jethro's daughter Zipporah, fathered two sons, and was a shepherd of Jethro's flocks when he encountered God speaking to him at the burning bush.

- Moses returned to Egypt without Zipporah and their sons.

- On their journey to the land of God's promise, the Israelites are encamped at the "mountain of God," which will become prominent in the following chapters. (Use a Bible map to show a possible location for the "mountain of God.")

- Apparently the Israelites are near Jethro's homeland, Midian. Jethro had heard "all that God had done for Moses and for his people Israel" (18:1). (Review

Jethro's words and actions in 18:10–12, which show a man who is not an Israelite respecting and worshiping the God of Abraham, Isaac, and Jacob.)

- Jethro observes Moses working from morning until evening, judging the disputes that the people have against one another.

- Jethro recommends to Moses that he appoint elders to deal with the minor disputes so that he need only deal with major issues.

- Moses listens to his father-in-law and follows his advice.

- Jethro departs and is never mentioned again in the Bible.

After summarizing Exodus 18 and the account of Jethro's visit with Moses, spend a few minutes discussing questions such as these:

- What are your impressions of the interactions between Jethro and Moses?

- What do you make of the account of a nonbeliever, who only heard others tell of their deliverance from Egypt, blessing and worshiping the God of the Israelites?

- What applications of Jethro's advice could we make today in terms of leadership in the church?

- Why do you think the author of Exodus inserted this account in the exodus narrative?

Closing

There are two possibilities for closing the session:

- If one or more persons in the group are comfortable leading the group in singing, sing the first two stanzas of the hymn "Guide Me, O Thou Great Jehovah." Have hymnals or a printout of the words available.

- Recite the following prayer or one that you have prepared:

Gracious God, we praise and thank you for your steadfast love that embraces us in all the seasons and circumstances of our lives. You have been faithful to your people in every generation as you provide the resources and the directions necessary to move toward the promise to which you call us. May our hunger and thirst for faith and life be satisfied by the bread of life and the living water that we know in Jesus, our savior, in whose name we pray. Amen.

AFTER THE SESSION

Encourage participants to read chapter 5 of the Participant's Guide, "Sinai and God's Covenant," and Exodus 19:1–21:11 and 24:1–18.

Exploring Manna/Bread and Water

Instructions: Your small group will work with one of the two sets of passages below. Read the Exodus passage and then read the Gospel passages. After reading the passages, spend a few minutes together answering the questions below.

Group 1: Focus on manna and the bread of life

Exodus 16:1–35

Matthew 6:9–13

Luke 22:13–20

John 6:1–15 and 22–40

Group 2: Focus on fresh water and living water

Exodus 15:22–25a and 17:1–7

Matthew 3:11–17 and 10:40–42

John 4:1–26 and 7:37–39

Questions:

1. What connections do you see between the Exodus passages and the Gospel passages?

   _____

   _____

2. How is it that Jesus can be seen as "the bread of life" and "living water"?

   _____

   _____

Session Five

Sinai and God's Covenant

A Study of Exodus 19:1–21:11; 24:1–18

BEFORE THE SESSION
Focus of the Session

The focus of this session is the giving of the Ten Commandments. Time will be spent considering the biblical concept of covenant, reviewing the setting of the event, and exploring the commandments in relation to selected teachings of Jesus.

Advance Preparation

- Read the selected portions of Exodus for this session.

- Read the comments and notes of the selected passage in a study Bible or commentary.

- Have on hand a Bible lands map so that you can show

the approximate location of Mount Sinai, where Moses and the Israelites received the Ten Commandments.

- Research covenant, theophany, Book of the Covenant, and blood sacrifice in a Bible dictionary, wordbook, or commentary.

- Write on a sheet of newsprint the response to the opening prayer.

- Obtain a recording or the lyrics of the song "On Eagles' Wings" to listen to or sing as part of the opening prayer.

- To prepare for the "Reviewing the Setting" section, spend some time with a study Bible and/or a Bible commentary so that you can provide brief explanations of each of the symbols.

- For the closing activity, gather enough magazines so that you have at least one per person. Select from *Time, Newsweek, People*, and others that have many articles, ads, and photos that can be used to illustrate the Ten Commandments.

- Have available a few extra Bibles for those who forget to bring one.

DURING THE SESSION
Opening Prayer

Introduce the session and the opening prayer by commenting on the focus for this session: the establishing of the covenant and giving of the Ten Commandments to Moses and the Israelites. The prayer is in the form of a litany and is based on portions of Exodus 19. The leader will read the following passages, and the group will respond in unison with, "Everything the LORD has spoken we will do" (v. 8). Have the words printed on a sheet of newsprint.

- "You have seen what I did to the Egyptians, and how I bore you on eagles' wings and brought you to myself" (v. 4).

- "Now therefore, if you obey my voice and keep my covenant, you shall be my treasured possession out of all the peoples" (v. 5).

- "Indeed, the whole earth is mine, but you shall be for me a priestly kingdom and a holy nation" (v. 6).

- "The LORD said to Moses, 'I am going to come to you in a dense cloud, in order that the people may hear when I speak with you and so trust you ever after'" (v. 9).

If you have the words for "On Eagles' Wings" or a recording of it, conclude the opening prayer by either listening to it, singing it, or reading the words.

Reviewing Session Four

Spend a few minutes reviewing the previous session for the sake of those who were not present and to take advantage of the reading everyone else did. Guide the review with the following questions:

- As they were beginning their journey through the wilderness, what were the Hebrews' complaints, and how did Moses and God respond to those complaints?

- What are some times and/or examples when we also have complaints against our leaders and/or God?

- Review the role of Jethro as he confronted Moses. What was Moses' situation or need?

- What advice did Jethro provide to Moses?

- How effective do you think that advice was?

- What are some ways we can apply that advice today?

Reviewing the Setting

Spend a few minutes reviewing the context in which Moses and the Israelites found themselves prior to receiving the Ten Words from God. Include in your review the following:

- Show on a Bible map an approximate location of Mount Sinai, where the Israelites are camped for a period of time. The site is also called Mount Horeb.

- Explain that Moses is the intermediary between God and the people of Israel.

- Invite participants to skim Exodus 19 to look for examples of God's power and presence and of God's being so holy that only Moses could address God in person. Ask for what they have found, and then discuss this question: "What does this suggest about the nature of God and God's relationship with humans?"

- Ask participants to skim Exodus 19 again to find all the symbolic acts: washing clothes, listening for trumpet sounds, avoiding sexual relations for three days, witnessing fire and shaking of the mountain, suffering penalty of death for touching the mountain, and hearing thunder. Explain briefly the significance or meaning of each of these symbols.

- Conclude by discussing one more question: "What do you see as the significance of all this preparation for receiving the Ten Words from God?"

Summarizing the Meaning of Covenant

In order to help participants understand the meaning of "covenant" in the context of Exodus 20, recall what March wrote in the Participant's Guide (pp. 40–42) as well as what you have found in your own study regarding the nature of "covenant." Be sure to include:

- the difference between the covenant with Abraham, Isaac, and Jacob and the covenant with the people of Israel at Mount Sinai;

- the difference between the covenant with Noah and the covenant at Sinai; and

- the meaning of "suzerainty covenant" and "apodictic laws."

Ask participants, "What are some ways the word 'covenant' is used today in legal matters? How is that meaning similar to or different from the biblical use of the word?"

Exploring the Ten Words from God

The exploring activity will proceed in several steps:

- Introduce the exploration of the Ten Commandments

by mentioning that in the Hebrew text they are known as the "Ten Words."

- Ask participants to name the Ten Commandments in order, without referring to their Bibles.

- Ask, "What are the differences between the first four commandments and the remaining six?"

- Direct everyone to turn to Matthew 5:17–20. Read in unison the passage, and then share a few of your insights regarding Jesus' interpretation of the law of Moses.

- Direct participants to the activity sheet "The Ten Commandments and Jesus' Teaching" on page 105 in the Leader's Guide.

- Divide the class into groups of two or three persons. Each group is to work with a different commandment and Gospel passage in order to answer the three questions.

- Gather as a whole group to share the findings of the small groups.

- Direct the group to Jesus' expression of the greatest commandment in Mark 12:28–34.

- Conclude by discussing one more question: "How does that passage sum up the meaning of the Ten Commandments and of Jesus' other teachings?"

Closing

There are two activities for closing the session. The first one will take about fifteen minutes. (If you don't think you will have that much time, tear out a number of photos, ads, and articles beforehand from which participants can select one or two.)

- Provide a stack of magazines (*Time, Newsweek, People,* etc.). Ask each person to select one of the Ten Commandments and to skim through the pages of a magazine to find one or more ads, photos, headlines, or articles that provide a contemporary visual expression of the selected commandment. After a few minutes, ask each person to share what he or she found and to explain how that illustrates in a positive or negative way the particular commandment. If you have ten or more participants, be sure that all ten of the commandments are covered. If you have fewer than ten participants but sufficient time, some may be able to focus on two commandments.

• Conclude the session by reciting together the Lord's Prayer.

AFTER THE SESSION

Encourage participants to read chapter 6 of the Participant's Guide, "Rebellion and Forgiveness," and Exodus 32:1–34:35.

The Ten Commandments and Jesus' Teachings

Instructions: Divide into groups of two or three. Each group will work with a different one of the following ten pairs of passages. Read the Gospel passage and reflect on any connections you see between it and the commandment as you consider the questions below.

Ten Commandments and Jesus' Teachings:

"You shall have no other gods" (20:2)	John 4:1–24
"You shall not make for yourself an idol" (20:4)	Matt. 23:16–24
"You shall not make wrongful use of the name of the LORD" (20:7)	Matt. 5:33–37
"Remember the Sabbath day, and keep it holy" (20:8)	Matt. 12:1–8
"Honor your father and mother" (20:12)	Matt. 15:1–9
"You shall not murder" (20:13)	Matt. 5:21–26
"You shall not commit adultery" (20:14)	Matt. 5:27–30
"You shall not steal" (20:15)	Luke 18:18–30
"You shall not bear false witness" (20:16)	Luke 18:18–30
"You shall not covet" (20:17)	Mark 4:13–20

Questions:

1. What connections do you see between the particular commandment and Jesus' teaching?

   _____

   _____

2. In what ways, if any, does it appear that Jesus reinterprets the commandment?

   _____

   _____

3. What do you sense to be Jesus' main point?

   _____

   _____

Session Six

Rebellion and Forgiveness

A Study of Exodus 32:1–34:35

BEFORE THE SESSION
Focus of the Session

The session will begin with a prayer of confession and assurance of forgiveness followed by enacting a readers' theater. The major topics of this session are the sin of the Israelites, the character of God, and the character of Moses, God's servant.

Advance Preparation

- Read the selected portions of Exodus for this session.

- Read the comments and notes of the selected passage in a study Bible or commentary.

- Research golden calf, forgiveness, and steadfast love (*chesed*) in a Bible dictionary, wordbook, or commentary.

- For an activity in which small groups will consider seven Old Testament passages reflecting on the character of God, either prepare an activity sheet or list on a sheet of newsprint the passages along with the question to discuss.

- Do the same for another activity in which participants will work again in groups of two or three to consider four passages that focus on the character of Moses.

- Write on a sheet of newsprint or a dry erase board the incomplete sentence suggested for the closing.

- Read the "After the Session" section to review the brief assignments for which you will need to seek volunteers in session 7.

- Provide a few extra Bibles for those who forget to bring one.

DURING THE SESSION
Opening Prayer

A major focus of this session is the rebellion of the people of Israel. They disobey the covenant that was established. They are so disobedient that God is ready to disown them. After Moses intercedes on their behalf, however, God relents and gives them another chance. There are times when we are also unfaithful and in need of God's forgiveness. The opening prayer follows the pattern of many churches' liturgies that include corporate prayers of confession followed by an assurance of forgiveness. The class will use a selection from Psalm 51 as a prayer of confession and a portion of Psalm 103 as the assurance of forgiveness.

- Direct participants to page 113 of the Leader's Guide, "Confession and Assurance of Forgiveness."

- Divide the group in two in order to read responsively the prayer of confession.

- Lead the group in reading in unison the assurance of forgiveness.

- After completing the opening prayer, guide a brief discussion with one question: "The psalms are from ancient times. How relevant do you think those words are for faith and life today?"

Reviewing Session Five

Spend a few minutes reviewing the previous session for the sake of those who were not present and to take advantage of the reading everyone else did. Guide the review with the following questions:

- The concept of covenant is featured in session 5. What are some insights you gained from last week's study of the covenant established with Moses and the people through the giving of the Ten Commandments?

- How would you summarize what you learned from the activity relating Jesus' teaching/interpretation to the Ten Commandments?

Setting the Stage

In order to establish a context for the discussion to follow, the group will participate in a readers' theater excerpted from Exodus 32–33.

- Direct participants to pages 114–15 of the Leader's Guide, "A Readers' Theater of Exodus 32:7–33:6."

- Ask for four volunteers for the roles of the LORD, the narrator, Aaron, and Joshua. The remaining persons in the group will read in unison the part of Moses.

- After completing the reading of the script, ask one question: "What are some insights or questions that came to you in this reading that you missed when you read the passage earlier?"

Reflecting on the Sin of the People

Spend a few minutes discussing the following questions or ones that you have created:

- What do you sense to be the motivation behind the people prevailing on Aaron to make a god of gold for them to worship?

- Why do you think Aaron was so willing to accede to the wishes of the people?

- What do you make of God saying to Moses, "Go down at once! Your people, whom you brought up out of the land of Egypt . . . " in which the people are identified as Moses' people instead of God's people?

- What is your interpretation or understanding of the phrase "stiff-necked people"?

- The Israelites were willing to give up their prized gold possessions in order to create the golden calf. What are some examples today of persons giving up prized "possessions" in order to create a god to worship?

Exploring the Character of God

The portions of Exodus in this session present a number of insights into the character of God. Ask participants to consider how God relates to the people by responding to these questions:

- After Moses had interceded with God on behalf of the people, Exodus 32:14 says, "And the LORD changed his mind about the disaster that he planned to bring to his people." What questions, comments, or affirmations do you have regarding Moses' attempt to persuade God to change God's mind?

- What are some other examples in Scripture showing God's willingness to change God's mind or heart?

Continue the discussion as follows:

- Read Exodus 34:6b–7 in unison. Invite persons with different translations of the Bible to share variations of the text.

- This brief passage presents God as one who is gracious and loving, merciful and forgiving. In the Participant's Guide (p. 49) March suggests that these attributes of God are reinforced in several other Old Testament passages. Form groups of two or three persons, and assign each group one of these passages.

  Numbers 14:13–20

  Nehemiah 9:16–21

Nehemiah 9:29–34

Psalm 86:8–15

Psalm 103:6–14

Joel 2:12–17

Jonah 3:10–4:5

Instruct each group to read its passage and to reflect on one question: "What do we learn about the character of God and God's relationship to the people in this passage?" After a few minutes, bring the small groups back together and ask them to share any insights they gained from reading and reflecting on their passage.

- Wrap up the consideration of the character of God by sharing with the group some of what you learned from your preparation related to the Hebrew word *chesed*, often translated as "steadfast love."

Considering the Character of Moses

From Exodus 3 forward, Moses is the main character in the drama of the exodus journey from Egypt to the promised land. Several of the passages studied for this session give significant insight into the nature of Moses as a man as well as his relationship with God. As in the previous activity, participants will work in groups of two or three persons. Guide them in the following steps:

- Introduce the activity by asking, "What are some impressions you have of Moses based on what we have studied to this point? What descriptive words would you use to speak about Moses?"

- Form four small groups and assign each group one of the following four passages that provide some particular insights into the character and roles of Moses. (If you have more than sixteen members of your class, additional small groups can work with the same passages.)

  Moses' encounter with God (32:7–20)

  Moses' encounter with Aaron (32:21–26)

  Moses' intercession with God (33:12–23)

  The shining face of Moses (34:27–35)

- Ask each group to read the passage and then discuss among themselves one question, "What insights do you gain from the passage regarding the character of Moses?

- After five to eight minutes, invite participants to join together as a whole group to share the insights they have discerned from their passages.

- Conclude this activity with discussion of one more question: "What can we learn from Moses that could make a difference in our faith journey with God and God's people?"

Closing

The closing for the session involves creating what can be described as an "instant litany" that can be formed by the following steps:

- Ask participants to complete a sentence that begins, "I understand God's steadfast love to mean . . ." (Display the incomplete sentence on a sheet of newsprint.) Give them about a minute to do so.

- After calling time, invite those who are willing to share their completed sentences. In response to each sentence, the whole group will say in unison, "Gracious God, we praise and thank you for loving us no matter what." (This response should also be visible on a sheet of newsprint.)

AFTER THE SESSION

The next session includes a lengthy, involved description of the tabernacle and some of the furnishings required to complete the tabernacle. Ask for five volunteers to do brief research on the topics listed below. (Assure participants that they can get sufficient information in about half an hour of searching on Wikipedia and other Web sites.) Reviewing the related pages in the Participant's Guide will also provide some information. In addition, they will be helped greatly if they have access to a study Bible. Ask the volunteers to make *brief* presentations in the next session. Give the following list with the related Exodus passages to the volunteers:

Ark of the covenant and mercy seat (25:10–22; 37:1–9)

Acacia wooden table and bread of the Presence (25:23–30; 37:10–16)

Six-branched lampstand (25:31–40; 37:17–24)

The altar of incense (30:1–10; 37:25–28)

The bronze basin (30:17–21; 37:29–38:8)

Also give the volunteers these directions for what to focus on for their reading and reporting:

- Describe briefly the object of your focus and its location in the tabernacle.

- If you are able to find and photocopy an image of the object, do so.

- Suggest what you think is the symbolic significance of the object.

Encourage participants to read chapter 7 of the Participant's Guide, "The Tabernacle and God's Presence," and Exodus 25:1–40; 26:30–37; 39:32–43; and 40:16–38.

Confession and Assurance of Forgiveness

Prayer of Confession (Ps. 51:1–12, responsively)

Have mercy on me, O God, according to your steadfast love;

according to your abundant mercy blot out my transgressions.

Wash me thoroughly from my iniquity, and cleanse me from my sin.

For I know my transgressions, and my sin is ever before me.

Against you, you alone, have I sinned, and done what is evil in your sight,

so that you are justified in your sentence and blameless when you pass judgment.

Indeed, I was born guilty, a sinner when my mother conceived me.

You desire truth in the inward being; therefore teach me wisdom in my secret heart.

Purge me with hyssop, and I shall be clean; wash me, and I shall be whiter than snow.

Let me hear joy and gladness; let the bones that you have crushed rejoice.

Hide your face from my sins, and blot out all my iniquities.

Create in me a clean heart, O God, and put a new and right spirit within me.

Do not cast me away from your presence, and do not take your holy spirit from me.

Restore to me the joy of your salvation, and sustain in me a willing spirit. Amen.

Assurance of Forgiveness (Ps. 103:10–13, in unison)

He does not deal with us according to our sins,

nor repay us according to our iniquities.

For as the heavens are high above the earth,

so great is his steadfast love toward those who fear him;

as far as the east is from the west,

so far he removes our transgressions from us.

As a father has compassion for his children,

so the LORD has compassion for those who fear him. Amen.

	A Readers' Theater of Exodus 32:7–33:6
Narrator:	Moses had been on the mountain with the LORD, receiving the tablets on which were written the Ten Words of the covenant. The LORD spoke to Moses.
The LORD:	Go down at once! Your people, whom you brought up out of the land of Egypt, have acted perversely; they have been quick to turn aside from the way that I commanded them; they have cast for themselves an image of a calf, and have worshiped it and sacrificed to it, and said, "These are your gods, O Israel, who brought you up out of the land of Egypt!" I have seen this people, how stiff-necked they are. Now let me alone, so that my wrath may burn hot against them and I may consume them; and of you I will make a great nation.
Narrator:	But Moses implored the LORD his God, and said,
Moses:	O LORD, why does your wrath burn hot against your people, whom you brought out of the land of Egypt with great power and with a mighty hand? Why should the Egyptians say, 'It was with evil intent that he brought them out to kill them in the mountains, and to consume them from the face of the earth'? Turn from your fierce wrath; change your mind and do not bring disaster on your people. Remember Abraham, Isaac, and Israel, your servants, how you swore to them by your own self, saying to them, "I will multiply your descendants like the stars of heaven, and all this land that I have promised I will give to your descendants, and they shall inherit it forever."
Narrator:	And the LORD changed his mind about the disaster that he planned to bring on his people. Then Moses turned and went down from the mountain, carrying the two tablets of the covenant in his hands, tablets that were written on both sides, written on the front and on the back. The tablets were the work of God, and the writing was the writing of God, engraved upon the tablets. When Joshua heard the noise of the people as they shouted, he said to Moses,
Joshua:	There is a noise of war in the camp.
Moses:	It is not the sound made by victors, or the sound made by losers; it is the sound of revelers that I hear.
Narrator:	As soon as he came near the camp and saw the calf and the dancing, Moses' anger burned hot, and he threw the tablets from his hands and broke them at the foot of the mountain. He took the calf that they had made, burned it with fire, ground it to powder, scattered it on the water, and made the Israelites drink it. Moses said to Aaron,
Moses:	What did this people do to you that you have brought so great a sin upon them?

Aaron:	Do not let the anger of my lord burn hot; you know the people, that they are bent on evil. They said to me, "Make us gods, who shall go before us; as for this Moses, the man who brought us up out of the land of Egypt, we do not know what has become of him." So I said to them, "Whoever has gold, take it off"; so they gave it to me, and I threw it into the fire, and out came this calf!
Narrator:	When Moses saw that the people were running wild (for Aaron had let them run wild, to the derision of their enemies), then Moses stood in the gate of the camp, and said,
Moses:	Who is on the LORD's side? Come to me!
Narrator:	And all the sons of Levi gathered around him. On the next day Moses said to the people,
Moses:	You have sinned a great sin. But now I will go up to the LORD; perhaps I can make atonement for your sin.
Narrator:	So Moses returned to the LORD and said,
Moses:	Alas, this people has sinned a great sin; they have made for themselves gods of gold. But now, if you will only forgive their sin—but if not, blot me out of the book that you have written.
The LORD:	Whoever has sinned against me I will blot out of my book. But now go, lead the people to the place about which I have spoken to you; see, my angel shall go in front of you. Nevertheless, when the day comes for punishment, I will punish them for their sin.
Narrator:	Then the LORD sent a plague on the people, because they made the calf—the one that Aaron made. The LORD said to Moses,
The LORD:	Go, leave this place, you and the people whom you have brought up out of the land of Egypt, and go to the land of which I swore to Abraham, Isaac, and Jacob, saying, "To your descendants I will give it." I will send an angel before you, and I will drive out the Canaanites, the Amorites, the Hittites, the Perizzites, the Hivites, and the Jebusites. Go up to a land flowing with milk and honey; but I will not go up among you, or I would consume you on the way, for you are a stiff-necked people.
Narrator:	When the people heard these harsh words, they mourned, and no one put on ornaments. For the LORD had said to Moses,
The LORD:	Say to the Israelites, "You are a stiff-necked people; if for a single moment I should go up among you, I would consume you. So now take off your ornaments, and I will decide what to do to you."
Narrator:	Therefore the Israelites stripped themselves of their ornaments, from Mount Horeb onward.

Session Seven

The Tabernacle
and God's Presence

*A Study of Exodus 25:1–40; 26:30–37; 39:32–43;
40:16–38*

BEFORE THE SESSION
Focus of the Session

The session will deal primarily with the construction of and furnishings for the tabernacle, as well as the experience of the Israelites as they moved from Mount Sinai through the desert wilderness to the promised land. In addition, there will be an activity for participants to compare tabernacle worship with passages from Psalms and several of the prophets that have a different perspective on worshiping God.

Advance Preparation

- Read the selected portions of Exodus for this session.

- Read the comments and notes of the selected passages
  in a study Bible or commentary.

- Research the tabernacle, the ark of the covenant, the mercy seat, cherubim, the temple, and the holy of holies in a Bible dictionary, wordbook, or commentary.

- For the opening prayer activity, list the seven Psalms passages that are suggested on a sheet of newsprint, and write out the unison response.

- Early in the week, check with the five volunteers who offered to make brief presentations later in this session to see if they were able to find any visuals of the object each was researching to share with the group. If any has not, offer to assist. You will find a number of examples on Wikipedia and other Web sites.

- Do a little research on the Internet to see if you can find any visualizations of the tabernacle to share with the group.

- Have on hand hymnals or copies of the words to the familiar hymn "Holy, Holy, Holy," which will be sung as part of the closing.

- Provide a few extra Bibles for those who forget to bring one.

DURING THE SESSION
Opening Prayer

A major emphasis of this session is on the worship of the Israelites, primarily that focused on the tabernacle. For the opening prayer, lead group members in the following activity, which features several psalms that also speak about the nature of worship by God's people:

- Invite participants to select one of the following passages to read:

    Psalm 22:22–28

    Psalm 27:4–9

    Psalm 30:1–5

    Psalm 40:4–8

    Psalm 95:1–7

    Psalm 99:4–9

- Instruct them to read the passage they chose and to reflect for a couple of minutes on what the passage communicates about the nature of worship.

- Invite participants to select a line or verse from the passage that speaks to them in a special way at this time.

- After a minute, ask them to take turns reading aloud the line or verse they chose. In response to each reading, the whole group will say in unison, "O God, we praise and honor you."

- When everyone has contributed, conclude with a discussion of this question: "When you look at the passage you read and the line or verse you shared, how relevant are those words to our faith and life today?"

Reviewing Session Six

Spend a few minutes reviewing the previous session for the sake of those who were not present and to take advantage of the reading everyone else did. Guide the review with the following questions, or ones you have created:

- What do you recall as the major points of last week's session, titled "Rebellion and Forgiveness"?

- We discussed the character of God. How would you summarize the character of God from that study?

- We also explored the character of Moses. Based on last week's study, as well as the previous five sessions, what phrases would you use to summarize what you think about Moses?

Setting the Stage

In order for participants to engage in the exploring activity that follows, it will be helpful to provide the following perspectives on the texts of this session's study:

- Remind participants of the points made by March in the Participant's Guide, page 54, "A Word about the Narrative Setting."

- Reinforce the point March made several times that much of what is included in Exodus regarding the construction of and furnishings for the tabernacle reflect more of what constituted the cultic life of the Israelites when they were settled in the promised land than what was experienced in the desert wilderness.

- Offer a few reflections on the distinctions between the tent of meeting, the tabernacle, and the temple.

- If you were able to find on the Internet a visualization of the tabernacle and made photocopies of it, share that with the group in order to set the stage for the brief presentations to follow.

Exploring the Tabernacle

Invite those who volunteered last session to make brief presentations this session to do so. The purpose of these presentations is to provide an overview of the tabernacle and its furnishings. The order for the presentations is as follows:

1. Ark of the covenant and mercy seat

2. Acacia wooden table and bread of the Presence

3. Six-branched lampstand

4. The altar of incense

5. The bronze basin

After the five presentations, ask if anyone has additional information to share about any of the five topics. Then ask a question: "What are some examples of furnishings in churches and/or synagogues today that serve similar purposes of representing the presence of God or the preparation of the worshiper to encounter God?"

Comparing Tabernacle Worship with Other Old Testament Texts

Through the presentations, the group will consider five particular items of the tabernacle furnishings that give clues to the role of the tabernacle in the worship life of the Israelites. The cultic life of the Israelites was quite formal and elaborate. In this next activity, participants will consider several other Old Testament passages that provide a counterpoint to worship in the tabernacle and later in the temple in Jerusalem. Guide the group in the following process:

- Direct participants to the resource sheet on page 122 of the Leader's Guide, "Comparing Old Testament Texts."

- Divide the class into five smaller groups.

- Assign each group one of the five passages.

- Read aloud the instructions, and answer any questions persons may have.

- Explain that each group will have about fifteen minutes to read its passage and answer the three questions.

After bringing the group back together, ask participants to give brief reports on the passage they considered. Conclude this activity by reflecting together on one more question: "What do you see as implications of these five passages regarding worship in our church today?"

Evaluating the Course

Say to the group, "We have spent a number of weeks together studying the book of Exodus. We have read the Participant's Guide and many chapters in Exodus, we have participated in a variety of activities together, and we have discussed many questions. It is impossible to remember all we have said and done together, but I am sure there are some things that are memorable from our study." Wrap up the course by leading the class in a discussion of as many of the following questions as you have time for:

- Of all the activities we did together, which ones were the most interesting, challenging, or helpful for you?

- What suggestions would you make for a future study like this one?

- What new insights have come to you as a result of this study of Exodus?

- How has this study contributed to your personal faith journey?

- Where do you hope that this study will lead you, our group, and/or our church?

Closing

Close the session and the course by doing the following:

- Read in unison Psalm 100, found on page 123 of the Leader's Guide.

- Sing or read the words of the familiar hymn "Holy, Holy, Holy."

Comparing Old Testament Texts

Instructions: Work in small groups. Each group will consider one of the following Old Testament passages. Read the passage and then discuss the questions below in light of the previous activity in which you focused on the tabernacle and its furnishings.

Old Testament Passages
Psalm 40:1–10
Isaiah 1:11–17
Jeremiah 7:16–26
Amos 5:18–24
Micah 6:1–8

Questions:

1. What do you sense to be the setting of the Old Testament text?

_____

_____

2. What do you think is the main point the psalmist or prophet is seeking to make?

_____

_____

3. How does this perspective on the type of worship God expects compare with what you have considered regarding worship in the tabernacle?

_____

_____

Psalm 100

Make a joyful noise to the LORD, all the earth.
Worship the LORD with gladness;
    come into his presence with singing.

Know that the LORD is God.
    It is he that made us, and we are his;
    we are his people, and the sheep of his pasture.

Enter his gates with thanksgiving,
    and his courts with praise.
    Give thanks to him, bless his name.

For the LORD is good;
    his steadfast love endures forever,
    and his faithfulness to all generations. Amen.

Appendix

Commentaries on Exodus

Fretheim, Terrence E. *Exodus*. Interpretation Bible Commentary for Teaching and Preaching. Louisville, KY: Westminster John Knox Press, 1991.

Janzen, J. Gerald. *Exodus*. Westminster Bible Companion. Louisville, KY: Westminster John Knox Press, 1997.

Meyers, Carol. *Exodus*. New Cambridge Bible Commentary. Cambridge: Cambridge University Press, 2005.

Newsome, James D. *Exodus*. Interpretation Bible Studies. Louisville, KY: Westminster John Knox, 1998.

Bible Study Aids

Achtemeier, Paul J., gen. ed. *The HarperCollins Bible Dictionary*. San Francisco: HarperCollins Publishers in consultation with the Society of Biblical Literature, 1996.

Frank, Harry Thomas, ed. *Atlas of the Bible Lands: New Edition*. Union, NJ: Hammond World Atlas Corp., 2007.

Mays, James L., gen. ed. *The HarperCollins Bible Commentary.* San Francisco: HarperCollins Publishers in consultation with the Society of Biblical Literature, 2000.

Nelson's Complete Book of Bible Maps and Charts. Nashville: Thomas Nelson Publishers, 1996.

Study Bibles

The Access Bible (NRSV). New York: Oxford University Press, 1999.

> Features include introductory articles for each book of the Bible; sidebar essays, maps, and charts in places appropriate to the text; section-by-section commentaries on the text; a glossary; a brief concordance; and a section of Bible maps in color.

The Discipleship Study Bible: New Revised Standard Version, including Apocrypha. Louisville, KY: Westminster John Knox Press, 2008.

> Features include introductory articles for each book of the Bible, study notes for key portions of each chapter of the Bible, a concise concordance, and helpful maps.

The Learning Bible (CEV). New York: American Bible Society, 2000.

> Features include introductory articles and outlines for each book of the Bible; fifteen background articles and over one hundred mini-articles; charts and timelines; a miniatlas; notes on biblical texts in six categories, each identified by a different color and symbol (geography; people and nations; objects, plants, and animals; ideas and concepts; history and culture; and cross-references); and hundreds of illustrations, photographs, and diagrams in color.

The New Interpreter's Study Bible: New Revised Standard Version with Apocrypha. Nashville: Abingdon Press, 2003.

> Features include introductory articles for each book of the Bible, extensive textual notes, many excursus essays, a helpful glossary, general articles related to biblical authority and interpretation, and colorful maps.

The NIV Study Bible (NIV). Grand Rapids: Zondervan, 1985.

> Features include introductory articles and outlines for each book of the Bible; extensive notes for explanation and interpretation of the biblical text on each page; helpful charts, maps, and diagrams within the biblical text; an index to subjects; a concise concordance; and a collection of maps in color.

CPSIA information can be obtained at www.ICGtesting.com
Printed in the USA
BVOW09s1234141215

430246BV00007B/35/P